Assaulted

Other Books By The Author

The Teacher Exodus: Reversing the Trend and Keeping Teachers in Classrooms (2018)
The Entitled Generation: Helping Teachers Teach and Reach the Minds and Hearts of Generation Z (2017)
Helping Parents Understand the Minds and Hearts of Generation Z (2017)
Common Sense Education: From Common Core to ESSA and Beyond (2016)
The Wrong Direction for Today's Schools: The Impact of Common Core on American Education (2015)
Teacher-Student Relationships: Crossing Into the Emotional, Physical, and Sexual Realms (2013)

Assaulted

Violence in Schools and What Needs to Be Done

Ernest J. Zarra III

ROWMAN & LITTLEFIELD
Lanham • Boulder • New York • London

Published by Rowman & Littlefield
An imprint of The Rowman & Littlefield Publishing Group, Inc.
4501 Forbes Boulevard, Suite 200, Lanham, Maryland 20706
www.rowman.com

Unit A, Whitacre Mews, 26-34 Stannary Street, London SE11 4AB

British Library Cataloguing in Publication Information Available

Library of Congress Cataloging-in-Publication Data

Library of Congress Cataloging-in-Publication Data Available

ISBN 978-1-4758-3980-7 (cloth : alk. paper)
ISBN 978-1-4758-3981-4 (pbk. : alk. paper)
ISBN 978-1-4758-3982-1 (electronic)

∞ ™ The paper used in this publication meets the minimum requirements of American National Standard for Information Sciences Permanence of Paper for Printed Library Materials, ANSI/NISO Z39.48-1992.

Printed in the United States of America

This book is dedicated to the teachers of America—particularly those who are survivors of violence against them. Continue to thrive, my friends and colleagues.

This book is dedicated to the teachers of America—particularly those who are survivors of violence against them. Continue to thrive, my friends and colleagues.

Contents

List of Tables

Foreword

Dr. Ernest J. Zarra III has written a provocative, yet must-read book for all teachers, administrators, and parents of students at all levels in education. *Assaulted! Violence in Schools and What Needs to Be Done*, should be a mandatory *read and respond assignment* for all K–12 educators, as well as many professors at the college level. Dr. Zarra's examination of the public school system of the United States, and the often hostile and volatile environments in which our educators are forced to work, should be of great interest to all education stakeholders.

As a retired California Peace Officer, parent of six children, and a volunteer high school football coach, I see the content of this book as a wake-up call. Parents, grandparents, and legal guardians of school students must come to terms with the changes in culture and our tendencies toward emotional escalation and violence. Some of these changes must include holding administrators responsible for what occurs on their campuses, as these occurrences lead to injuries of those serving in the classrooms under their tutelage.

All readers should keep in mind that educators in our public schools are responsible for the development of our future generations. Their individual successes, when added together, comprise the corporate success of the nation. At this time in our nation's history, the success of our nation must be front and center—and teachers are on the frontlines as gatekeepers of this success. That being said, teachers need our help now more than ever to protect them in their livelihood. This is where Dr. Zarra steps in.

With careful research and sensibility Zarra identifies the deeply rooted causes of the structural deterioration of public education, the frustrations of the individual teacher, and the education system in whole. He also allows the research to lead the reader to some logical conclusions. One of these conclu-

sions is that teaching in schools today has become more physically dangerous than in previous decades.

Comparatively, most modern administrators and political purveyors of
higher education would consider the educator of the last century to be rudi-
mentary in developmental skills, politically incorrect, and completely inca-
pable of educating our future generation to any level of success. Dr. Zarra
draws out these comparisons and alludes to the notion that teachers of the
past were more successful, in part because they relied on fundamentals
rooted in discipline both at home and at school.

Although schools today have similar structures as schools of the past,
fundamental, cultural discipline is missing. The American family is fractured
and many students are needy and frustrated. Sometimes these frustrations are
demonstrated by lashing out in ways unprecedented for students in the past.

Most school districts in America prohibit serious disciplinary actions, in
order to satisfy political and legal decisions. The law has placed students at
the center of the education universe and enables them, while clothed with
impunity. Discipline is truly the cornerstone of all learning and is not option-
al. Without it, behavioral accountability is left to the devices of the students.
Therein lies one of the serious issues of today's school culture.

Dr. Zarra addresses the *need* for better discipline in schools, so that teachers can feel safe, students are nurtured in a protected environment, and learning can occur without fear. The data are clear. Diminishing discipline in our
schools has resulted in the development of a mob mentality, over time. This
mentality leads to brazen actions often resulting in violence in schools—
including violence against teachers.

Teachers trying to work around the students who wish to control the
classrooms find that they are constrained. Students are allowed to waste time,
money, and talents. The rise of violence in classrooms has become a threat
and must be met accordingly. From a law enforcement perspective, *assaults
are defined as physical attempts to cause bodily harm.* The actual instance of
inflicting bodily injury is defined as battery. Students are causing injuries to
teachers by the commission of both. Dr. Zarra provides numerous examples
of both assaults and batteries throughout the book.

For the record, ascending levels of assault are based on the instrument
utilized in the injurious attempt, such as the use of hands, fists, objects, etc.
Levels of battery are based on the severity of the injuries inflicted, and range
from everything superficial, to great bodily injury, and death. Americans
should be highly concerned that such discussions should reference our public
schools.

In assault and/or battery incidents which occur in group settings, there
usually are secondary and tertiary victims. Dr. Zarra aptly points out these
effects of violence in classrooms, especially the effects upon students after
watching their teacher assaulted. He shares many anecdotes of direct and

indirect impacts upon others, including physical and emotional responses. This is called *the secondhand smoke syndrome!* Everyone is affected by a disruptive force, like a pebble in the middle of a calm body of water.

Immediate action has to be taken to stop a violent act in any setting, especially in a place of learning. Those who minimize such violence, or excuse behaviors that injure, because of a program or policy are defying the agreement for safety and trust which parents have every right to expect. There must be order. Dr. Zarra keenly points this out in many chapters.

Zarra also brings into the discussion the vulnerability and helplessness many teachers feel, by not having the support of their school-site and district-level administrators. He is right on point when he states that educators are unable to maintain order, this results in a sense of helplessness in students as they fear for their own safety. After all, if the teacher cannot protect students, what are students to do to protect themselves?

Zarra has thought this through and offers what he thinks is a starting point for students to own their classroom setting. He describes a classroom management model by the title *Crowd-Friending*. Elementary students, especially, can step up to regain the emotional and actual power in a classroom by exercising a model such as described by the author.

Assaulted! outlines root causes of many unacceptable acts of violence against our educators. The book also provides shocking evidence of the repugnant reality that violence is quickly becoming a norm in our schools. Since when is it part of a teacher's job requirement to be assaulted? Whether in America, or any other nation, when did violence become the problem of the individual teacher, and not an issue for the entire education system? Dr. Zarra traces several of the issues that have resulted in both American and International education arriving at this frightening place.

If teachers are meant to be in the line of potential violence and injury, it may be time for all educators to learn the verbal skills taught to law enforcement officers, as a means to de-escalate situations before they become violent. If not, there must be serious intervention incorporated into teacher education programs.

Teachers must understand that special needs and special education students may require different handling than the rest of the students. Dr. Zarra addresses intervention as if he anticipated its need in today's diverse public school classrooms.

Today's educators should be sufficiently trained and equipped with a quick plan to respond and de-escalate potentially violent situations in the class room and school yard. Although not all situations can be foreseen, that which is viewed as predictable, may also prove as highly preventable.

Zarra brilliantly highlights that disruptions of the daily educational process, however slight they may be, cannot be left uncorrected. Perpetrators' actions must result in punishment commensurate with the acts committed. In striking a balance, this book also includes a chapter on teachers fighting back and assaulting students.

As shameful as this is to education, teachers are sexually, physically, and verbally assaulting students in increasing numbers. Therefore, not only are students committing violence against teachers, but teachers are also assaulting students. Zarra takes on both of these problems in this book. Add to this the additional assaults upon teachers, by parents, and the toxicity that exists in today's public school environment is at crisis levels.

Zarra is not shy in bringing up several sensitive topics. The issues associated with mainstreaming of special needs students and various aspects of race theory and violence are approached honestly and cogently. Accordingly, when discipline is warranted, it must be dealt with swiftly and fairly, regardless the demographic. All students are exactly that—students!

Zarra reveals the shocking internal aspects of assaults on teachers. Crimes against teachers are crimes against the state and therefore should fall beyond the scope of school administrative authority. They should always be matters for courts of law. However, these crimes must be reported. Here is where administrators must step up and do the right thing.

Likewise, there must be civil avenues for teachers to file law suits swiftly and easily, so as to protect their professional careers. They will most likely never receive a monetary settlement from this action, however it will deter slanderously outrageous claims and false allegations. In this age of recording devices and social media, teachers and students can both become viral sensations for all the wrong reasons.

Educators should be briefed quarterly, or when a significant court case is decided in favor of teachers. Like any other citizen of the United States, teachers must have the right to self-defense, in protecting themselves and their students. Obviously, teachers must never be the aggressors. Are we at the point now where all-day video-recording and video surveillance should join canine searches and metal detectors on school campuses, in order to protect our teachers and students?

In conclusion, I highly recommend this book. As a retired peace officer, and as one who volunteers time with teenagers and families, I commend Dr. Zarra for his important and seminal work on the very important issues of teacher and student safety.

Joel Brock, Retired Peace Officer
California Highway Patrol
January 6, 2018

Acknowledgments

An idea that becomes a proposal and eventually turns into a book . . . that sounds like an easy process to undertake. But writing a book is a labor of love and more an endurance than an undertaking. Besides, as I age, I hope to avoid anything to do with *undertaking* for a good, long while.

The brave teachers who speak out about the violence they experience from their students, their parents, and anyone else seeking to harm them on the job are heroes. They are heroes in my book and heroes in *this* book. I want to honor those with the courage to speak out and acknowledge the difficulty in stepping forward, especially during this time of cultural and education policy change.

I could not have written this book without the assistance of my educator friends, both local and around the nation. Some of you are victims of violence and have overcome these incidents. Your encouragement and inspiration are the reasons our schools still have a chance to reverse some of the trends that tend to beset our success as educators. You make a difference each day you step into the potential risky situations.

Many thanks go out to the readers and reviewers of my work. Your insights are invaluable, and your delicate approach to a sensitive topic is most appreciated.

Last, I acknowledge and thank my life partner, Suzi, my wife and a survivor of school violence on multiple occasions. Thank you for understanding yet again that time to research and write are paramount to putting together a book for publication. Thank you for being strong enough to endure the pains of both a career and an educator–author husband. You have the patience of a saint. I trust this is a vicarious catharsis for all those victimized by violence on the job.

Introduction

The purpose of this book is to provide the reader with an understanding of a massive and evolving problem in schools today. Recently, I wrote a book about Common Core and how I believe it to be *The Wrong Direction for Today's Schools*. I also penned the book *Common Sense Education*. The concerns raised in those books persist to this day. But concerns evolve.

Aside from analyzing low rankings on international comparative assessments, the decline of overall literacy scores, and issues such as these, I decided to examine another set of problems affecting our schools. This set pertains much less to academics and more to the issues of safety for teachers and students.

The problems that are the focus of this book are the causes and outbreaks of violence, particularly against teachers. But they also include teachers assaulting students. The fact is there are increases in violence on school campuses all over America, and not just on public school campuses either.

There are reasons for this violence and its continuing increase. The causes range from person to person and demographic to demographic. No one would disagree that there have always been problems in America's public schools that needed immediate attention. However, no one problem is more pressing than keeping teachers and students physically safe.

Schools are supposed to be havens of protection. So are our homes. Yet violence seems to touch and affect all Americans today in frightening fashion. Violence at school places the nation's teachers and students at greater risk of physical injury, and even death. Schools have become the ultimate of soft targets. Teaching and learning cannot be accomplished in environments of fear. Our havens have turned to places of aggression, remonstration, and distress.

In the midst of the research about violence against teachers at schools—and there is plenty of it throughout the book—another issue came to light. Sadly, another frightening phenomenon is arising: *teachers assaulting students*.

I encourage the reader to investigate the issues discussed in this book in an effort to discover why these issues occur now in history. Check out the research, pay attention to the news, read interviews and surveys of teachers, and draw your own conclusions. Readers are also encouraged to check with local teachers. In doing so, empathy might yield to consternation and shock.

I believe I am a realist with nearly forty years in the education field. I have served in K–12 and taught at the college and postgraduate levels. I have also trained teachers across generations, many of whom are gainfully employed and marking their time in the profession at the time of this writing. They seek to make a difference each day, as most teachers do. I am proud to have had such a storied career in education, and I do not count myself out of the equation, just yet.

To the point of relevance, this book is meant to draw all readers toward understanding there are serious problems of violence in our schools. The book is not another antibullying book. Those have their place in education. This book should be used as an informational tool for those presently in education and those anticipating a career in the profession. The many suggested solutions offer the reader some refreshing ideas in terms of what needs to be done about the violence.

Formal and informal surveys are discussed within several chapters. I conducted an informal national survey in an attempt to gather data for additional analysis. The data appear in the book, and the detailed survey results appear in the appendix. Along with the surveys are comments from teachers and personal anecdotes. The reader will be both enthralled and intrigued, and many teachers and professors will see themselves in the data and the anecdotes.

THE STRUCTURE OF THE BOOK

The overall structure of the book is six chapters in length; it is laid out for the reader to understand the nature of the problems of violence in schools. Many sections and subsections carry the reader through each chapter. At the close of each of the six chapters, the reader will see a section about what needs to be done to assist schools in stemming the violence that takes place.

Chapter 1 defines the problem of school violence and describes it in terms of the types of assaults that occur. The chapter also addresses why so many teachers feel unsafe in their classrooms and analyzes the reasons teachers are leaving the classrooms for good. The problem of violence in schools is not just an American problem, and Chapter 1 illustrates this clearly.

Violence has *reasons*. There are causes and effects pertaining to violent outbursts in classrooms. The *seeds* of this violence are explored and discussed. The chapter ends with a summary of survey data and anecdotes, which will engage the reader on a more personal level.

Chapter 2 explores the extent of the problems of violence in schools, the forms of this violence in our schools, and the duress that teachers are under on a regular basis. The chapter also reveals why teachers minimize violence in their classrooms and are afraid to report it. The chapter concludes with what needs to be done to reduce violence in America's schools.

Chapter 3 examines *hands-off policies* toward students committing violence and the expectations placed on teachers to reduce violence, especially among students of color, some of whom happen to be categorized as special needs. The main question asked is whether teaching has become a *contact sport*. Zero-tolerance policies are also revisited in this chapter as deterrents.

Chapter 4 takes a hard look at the pandemic of students assaulting teachers. This problem is not relegated to the United States. Teachers around the world are dealing with violence against them. This chapter analyzes students today in terms of some cultural clashes and provides reasons for the violence that occurs. There is a lengthy section on actual teacher assaults, and the chapter concludes with what needs to be done to combat these assaults.

Chapter 5 addresses the programs and practices of mainstreaming and challenges the reader to examine the possible connections of increases in violence and students mainstreamed in regular education classes. There are differences between *special education* students and those considered as *special needs*. The reader will come to understand these differences and be asked to consider why so many students of special needs designations are now matriculated in regular education classrooms.

The reader will also be made aware of the increase in violence in regular education classrooms on the parts of students with behavioral and emotional disorders as well as mental illnesses and what steps can be taken to diminish these incidents.

Chapter 6 is an examination of teacher violence *against* students. It includes real stories of sexual, physical, emotional, and verbal assaults by teachers upon students. This trend is disturbing, and there are reasons for it. These reasons are examined in this chapter. The chapter closes with state codes of conduct for teachers and a glimpse into what is taking place at several prestigious colleges to stem the tide of sexual assaults and false allegations. The rise in inappropriate teacher–student relationships is addressed along with what needs to be done to regain a balance of boundaries.

I trust the reader is informed by the research, assisted by the suggestions, and motivated by what needs to be done. Violence in our schools is unacceptable, and it is time to bring the problem out into the open and begin serious discussions on just what needs to be done about it. Our nation is not only losing teachers for the classrooms; we are losing the very soul of education by allowing violence to affect the minds and hearts of our students.

Chapter One

The Problem of Violence in Schools

A century ago, teachers were almost certainly among the most educated members of their communities. This meant that they were to some extent looked up to because of their learning (although they were looked down upon because they didn't do "honest work"). Today, the education levels of teachers are perceived to be much the same as most of the community in large part because so many members of society have finished high school and even beyond. Accordingly, teachers are no longer looked up to because of their education. They are, however, still looked down upon to some extent because they don't work 9-to-5 jobs and they have so many holidays. [1]

The topic of assault is not an easy topic to address. How much more difficult does it become when considering children as perpetrators of violence? Unfortunately, it has become necessary. Teachers are being assaulted every day. [2] What exactly is meant when it is reported that a teacher is assaulted, and what actions equate to assault?

It would be fair to say that any definition of assault would denote some sort of physical altercation. Yet this is not necessarily the case. There are other actions and experiences that are categorized as assaults as well. Defining the term and the problems are very important.

DEFINITION OF THE PROBLEM

In terms of this book, physical acts of assault are described as *primary assaults*. These types of assaults usually bring some harm upon a person, which may result in injury and may include personal property damage. These assaults are often viewed as more serious than secondary assaults.

Secondary assaults are categorized as assaults upon a person's emotions, well-being, reputation, ability to work, or career in general. Secondary assaults may occur by berating with words, threats, or verbal confrontations. Online social media posts are examples of secondary assaults, and they are often classified by law as simple assaults, where physical touching does not have to be included.

PRIMARY AND SECONDARY ASSAULTS

Primary and secondary categories of assaults are addressed within the pages of this book. The evidence is presented via cases, reports, personal anecdotes, and analyses of national and international surveys. The data point to the following five distinctions of primary and secondary assaults, which are to be considered to be forms of violence in today's schools:

- *Physical:* Examples of these types of assaults include hitting, slapping, punching, and kicking. These also include being spit on, hurt with objects, or thrown or manipulated by hand or destroying property.
- *Sexual:* Examples of sexual assaults include sexual harassment or implicit and explicit sexual requests and acts of sexual or intimate contact. Sexual assaults may very well involve other forms of assaults.
- *Verbal:* Examples of these types of assaults include profanity and belligerence, verbal tirades, spoken threats of bodily harm or property damage, or sexual requests.
- *Emotional:* Examples of these types of assaults are persistent name-calling and belittling as well as the incitement of emotional reactions in response to student behaviors.
- *Social:* Examples of these types of assaults include social media posts, sharing of photos and texts through smartphone apps, clandestinely recording classes with the intent to embarrass or blackmail, and exacerbating instances at school by gossip. Attempts at character assassination, career ruination, or online bullying are also included.

Definition of Violence

Assaults do not happen in a vacuum, and there are causes and effects associated with the acts. The acts are considered violent if the definition of violence is satisfied. Violence, then, is defined as "the use of physical force so as to injure, abuse, damage, or destroy; injury by or as if by distortion, infringement, or profanation; vehement feeling or expression."[3] In this definition there is a built-in cause-and-effect relationship.

In any discussion concerning assaults, there should be some consideration given to distinguishing between actions causing accidental injuries and premeditated actions causing injuries. For example, in education, administrators are sometimes reluctant to identify student attacks as willful and intentional and sometimes talk teachers down from the emotional first responses of assuming motivation.

Actions stemming from anger are handled differently in schools, especially if these actions stem from special needs or special education students. These special *incidents* are discussed at length in chapters 4 and 5. Teachers are instructed today not to rush to judgment. Rather, teachers are strongly encouraged to look more deeply and empathetically into the reasons for students' actions and not just at the actions themselves.

ACCIDENTS OR INCIDENTS?

Some assaults are deemed "accidental," even when serious injuries occur to the teacher. Teachers absorb many injuries throughout the year as part of the incidentals of their jobs. What is being overlooked is that many of these incidents are reportable as assaults but are not officially written up. In an era when administrators are under a mandate to reduce suspensions and expulsions, there appears to be a higher tolerance of student assaults upon teachers than tolerated in the past. This reality is driven by both policy and practice.

It befuddles the mind to think that during this period of time, when mandatory reporter laws are in effect, teachers would be asked to withhold writing up and reporting assaults upon them. If informed, are not administrators bound by the same reporter laws as teachers?

Many physical altercations experienced by teachers are not accidental. There are legal terms that may apply criminality toward certain actions, such as assault, battery, abusive language, and the newer phenomena of online threats and emotional coercion, known as bullying.

It is not cliché to assert that the Internet has changed the "games" of bullying and character assaults. Both teachers and students—and some parents—are willing participants in these assaults. Some extreme actions result from the joint actions of assault by these participants.[4] Many of these are chronicled in this chapter and others.

Students are using social media in targeted ways to bully fellow students. They are also using social media to threaten and coerce teachers. Teachers must be trained to handle these power plays by students and parents.[5] As if to make matters worse, teachers who cross the line with students are often on a collision course with ruination of reputation, a loss of career, restriction of freedom, and usually rejection by family members. For additional information on this problem and an understanding of the nature of its causes, as well as some solutions, see *Teacher-Student Relationships: Crossing into the Emotional, Physical, and Sexual Realms.*[6]

SEEDS OF VIOLENCE

Teachers run the risk of being assaulted when they step into the hornets' nests of emotions that sometimes rise to fever pitch throughout the day at school. Stepping in at the wrong moment could result in injury to the teacher. If they fight back, they risk losing their jobs. In a recent case involving a physics teacher, a student body-slammed the instructor and the instructor did nothing to defend himself. He was fearful of losing his job.[7]

Generational differences may prompt students to lash out at teachers. Expectations of Baby Boomers and Generation X teachers differ from expectations of Millennial teachers and Generation Z's newer teachers. Younger parents are rearing their children with different sets of values than their parents before them. At the root of today's values appears a general sense of cultural coarseness. Rage-oriented expressions seem quite prevalent today as well. Social media is beginning to take its toll on a generation.

The Obama Administration

The federal government during the Obama administration made a point to focus on its "controversial campaign by progressives."[8] President Obama implemented executive orders and policies making stipulations on graduation rates to counter what the administration deemed as disproportionate suspension and expulsion rates for minority students in high schools in America. Even those with records of violence were to be considered differently.

As the winds of politics shifted, the current Secretary of Education, Betsy DeVos, and some teacher groups favored a repeal of measures billed as "disciplinary protection for minority students,"[9] while other teachers did not support the repeal. Deep divisions persist over this issue. For example, the Legal Aid Justice Center alleged in 2017 that "African-American students make up about 23 percent of the public school enrollment, but they account for 60 percent of the suspensions."[10]

Some critics believe the Obama orders planted seeds for altercations and assaults in high schools by not enforcing school policy fairly across school demographics.[11] One of the main concerns after the implementation of the order was the extent that teachers could expect to hold students accountable for learning and adherence to behavioral standards. Such expectations expressed were causes of additional concerns.

A Free Pass

An example of this changing set of values occurred in 2016 at Johnson High School in St. Paul, Minnesota. A teacher was breaking up a girl fight and was punched in the head from behind. The student who assaulted the teacher was a male student who was "upset that [the teacher] had put his hands on the girls"[12] to break up the fight. Hitting teachers does not always bring swift consequences today.

Teachers at the Minnesota high school say "the incident is emblematic of how disruption and violence has gotten out of control since Superintendent Valeria Silva took over the St. Paul schools in 2009 with a focus on reducing suspensions for minority students. The goal was to reduce discrepancies in suspension numbers between White and Black students,[13] which occurs in some cities.[14]

"Teachers believe that in the name of better stats, Silva enacted discipline policies that effectively gave students a free pass when they cussed out staff or bullied their peers. As a result, these problems had ballooned into several high-profile assaults"[15] over the past few years at several high schools under Silva's leadership.

During the 2015–2016 school year, "Minneapolis Public Schools . . . reported 986 K-5 suspensions/exclusions/expulsions, while the numbers in the St. Paul public school district were even higher: 1,833—the most in Minnesota."[16] Lately, there has been movement toward setting up policies in school districts that call for suspensions, exclusions, or expulsions for violence only. This policy would not consider what is described as nonviolent behaviors. Nonviolent behaviors are sexual harassment, theft, bullying, and several others. As one blogger commented:

> I don't mean to mock alternative means of improving behavior, which I support wherever possible. My concern comes from [the] disastrous tenure of Valeria Silva's time as superintendent, where teachers were dis-empowered in their own classrooms and disruptive kids were kept in class without consequence, ruining class for everyone. The choice was between removing the one or two disruptive kids from class, or making class meaningless for the other 30. The no-discipline policy was implemented because the kids pulled out were disproportionately African-American. But keeping them in class didn't help them, and it hurt the other kids, over 70 percent of whom were non-white at the school at the time.[17]

QUICK FUSES AND LACK OF SELF-CONTROL

There seem to be quick fuses on the parts of peoples' emotions, in general. In Philadelphia, Pennsylvania, a sixteen-year-old student was late to one of his classes, which prompted an argument between him and one of his teachers. The result of the argument was recorded by a student at the end of the period. "Fists were raised and the student threw the first punch."[18] Police were called, and the teacher told them he had tried to "call security from his classroom but was unable to get help, and had to get stitches after the fight."[19]

Even some kindergartners are joining in to assault teachers. As an example, in 2015, a Pittsburgh, Pennsylvania, kindergarten student continued "to act out at a western Pennsylvania elementary school, despite efforts including a 'cooling off' space and extra staff hired to deal with unruly students who allegedly attacked at least 11 teachers."[20] The principal at the school had been placed on paid leave, and "replaced in the wake of complaints that he didn't act to stop the incidents."[21]

Four teachers and the school librarian have since resigned from the Pittsburgh elementary school because of the increase in physical violence. This increase was due in part to some special needs students who were mainstreamed without adequate full-time aides. Students in schools across America have grabbed teachers' necks; kicked, bitten, and scratched them; and thrown objects at them in anger. The incidents described at the Pittsburgh elementary school are not an exception. Today's kindergarten teachers have to "constantly worry about their safety."[22]

On the brighter side, teachers in Allentown, Pennsylvania, agreed to a new contract with the Allentown School District. The new contract "protects teachers who have been assaulted by students."[23] In addition to raising salaries for teachers, the contract contains "a unique assault protection provision that provides association members protection from students who have assaulted them."[24] This is a good first step.

A few of the options in the contract to protect teachers include the provision that "a teacher who's assaulted cannot be asked to teach that student in a classroom or supervise them in another capacity." However, this does not apply to "encounters in hallways, cafeterias, bus duties or other general supervision over large groups of students."[25]

There are many questions that must be asked and answered. Some of these questions are both difficult to ask and probably even more difficult to answer. One roadblock to addressing both are the roles that bureaucracy and politics play in any given state. The fact is that some state policies might actually lead to increases in assaults.[26]

HANDS-OFF POLICIES LEAD TO ASSAULTS

In 2012, a state policy in Maine that limited teachers from restraining students in classes seems to have backfired. Since the adoption of the policy, the Maine Education Association teachers reported that there had been "dozens of instances" of teachers "being assaulted by students." Apparently, major disruptions have occurred in school due to the policy. For example, in the Portland area, a high school was evacuated twice because of a student who had to be isolated.[27]

Another example from Maine includes the dispatching of five adults to spend time talking with a kindergartner who refused to obey and leave the playground to return to class and a student damaging school property. Are schools willing to sacrifice property damage just to allow a student space to express his or her anger when restraining would have been the best course of action? Consider a school policy that would allow an unrestrained sixth-grade student to cause "$1,000 worth of damage to a school cafeteria"[28] or another angrily using a tool "to dig a hole in a wall"[29] or destroy a classroom phone.

Revisions of policies such as these are being requested by teachers' associations and unions in some thirty states due to the vagueness associated with what is determined as an emergency. Questions are being explored as to when it may be deemed appropriate to restrain a violent student and when restraint can avoid escalating outbursts, causing other serious concerns.

What they seek in each instance are changes in state laws that "allow more flexibility for teachers who deal with out-of-control students."[30] There are more than whispers about hands-off policies leading to more violence in public schools. The fallout from this is rippling across the nation. In the Bakersfield City School District, in Bakersfield, California, "Teachers have been slapped, pushed and had eggs thrown at them in class, yet students are rarely suspended or expelled."[31]

PERSONAL ANECDOTES

Sometimes, injuries upon teachers are serious and need medical attention. Sometimes, the injuries show up later. Even with declining medical attention, there is always some form of injury. The following experiences of this author and his colleagues illustrate a few of the many reasons for this book.

Anecdote #1: The Special Needs Student

On a personal note, a few years back, a student was standing outside a faculty restroom at the school at which I was employed. The student was on his cell phone, which was against the rules at the time. So asking for his cell phone to be put away resulted in a refusal. The student was supposedly speaking with his father. I reminded him of the rules so that father could also hear, and the student disregarded my instructions.

As the student finally finished his phone call, I asked for the phone, and the student became enraged. He reluctantly handed it over because those were the rules. As I turned my back to enter the faculty restroom, the student ran at me and shoved me into a stucco wall, resulting in a few scrapes, which drew blood. Immediately, I heard distant voices yell, "No, don't!"

I was uncertain as to whether those voices were directed at the student or at what the people perceived I might do in response to being assaulted. Fortunately, I quickly realized what I was dealing with and that faculty members of the special education department were the people yelling in my direction. It turned out that members of that department had witnessed the assault.

I decided not to have the student arrested, but I documented some of the loopholes and inconsistencies of special education discipline. I moved on, as most teachers do, because the daily grind summons our energies and attention.

One month after the incident, the special education student approached me with a special education teacher by his side and apologized for his actions on that day. He explained that he and his father were arguing on the phone. Just another example as to why being technologically connected to friends and parents all day is not in the students' or teachers' best interests. In some strange way, it seemed that the boy's father had played a role in my assault. Nevertheless, we had a wonderful moment of forgiveness and restoration. A special education student learned the powerful value of asking for and receiving forgiveness.

I often wonder what would have happened if I had retaliated and taken him to the ground. Being under control of one's emotions in difficult situations is very important for teachers—even in the middle of an assault. That is not to say that the next time, with a different student, things might work out differently—including a lawsuit against the student and the family.

The good news is that courts are beginning to side with teachers who bring suits against the families and the students. However, most districts cannot be sued successfully over incidents like the one described. Often, it is written in collective bargaining agreements that arbitration and mediation are the avenues for association and district issues, often including teacher assaults that result from hostile working conditions.

Anecdote #2: Inclusion Gone Bad

Writing as the spouse of an elementary teacher who was assaulted repeatedly by an elementary school special needs student during the 2016–2017 school year, I can verify that the mental and emotional stress is real. The physical and psychological aftereffects of external injuries linger for months. My wife was given six special needs students in a class of twenty-nine students. She was expected to teach her second-grade class, with 21 percent of her class designated as special needs. She was to do all this without any full-time aides for mainstreamed special needs students.

Three of the students in question had brain disorders, two of the students were extremely violent, and one should have been designated as a special day student. Their special needs ranged from autism to serious learning, processing, and emotional and behavioral disorders.

One of these six students liked to throw things at people, including scissors, chairs, and desks; stab people with pencils; heave books across rooms; and threaten to kill many in the class—including my wife.

One day, this violent second-grade student punched my wife in the stomach and twisted her wrist, causing a severe injury. The result of this assault caused her to go to an urgent care facility directly. These assaults and injuries continued with others, including injuring a school psychologist, yard duty aides, and classmates—both in and outside of class. Things became so bad that my wife's class would run to the safe corners of the room if the violent student began lashing out.

My wife was directed to call for help when she needed it. When that did not provide relief, she was asked to change the way she dealt with the student, using only positive statements. The joke around our home became "Nice going, buddy! You really demonstrated excellent violence today in class."

An initial district grievance was filed after meetings with the district superintendent, school principal, and my wife's association representative. She was promised by the administration that the student would be moved since she felt unsafe with him in the classroom. The principal was known for his enabling of hostile workplaces, favoritism toward select teachers with whom he was involved intimately, and a general lack of support for all others. No one was surprised when the principal eventually refused to move the student, reneging on his promise.

The student continued to assault others, and the principal just allowed the year to expire. To press matters further, my wife submitted an official second grievance against the school principal for allowing a hostile workplace. She was eventually compensated for her injuries and time away from work.

Anecdote #3: Felt Like a Prison

In 2005, while on a school visitation in Los Angeles, our visitation team was introduced to an energetic and motivated secondary principal. Some of the reasons for this visitation was that this secondary school had earned Distinguished School honors and it had an open invitation to visit and examine the reasons for its academic success.

The truth was that the school's standardized test scores were extremely high. This was during the era of No Child Left Behind, and assessments were considered high stakes because of the importance placed on each school's Academic Performance Index (API). In March 2017, the state of California replaced API with a new set of evaluation criteria.[32] Naturally, any school that raised scores to very high levels during the high stakes era snagged the curiosity of other school administrators.

Our visitation team thought it odd that we were literally locked into the library by campus security. Curiosity getting the better of some of us, we asked to use the restroom so we could scope out students and the wider school culture. Security was summoned to the library, and we were escorted to restrooms for faculty, some fifty yards from the library.

On the way through the hallways, both security and the visitation team were sworn at, sexually harassed, and bombarded with projectiles. Security did nothing to intervene. Essentially, all of us were verbally harassed and physically assaulted with debris. The women were specifically sexually harassed. At the end of our day at the school, we were reminded that this secondary school was one of the best in the Los Angeles area.

Anecdote #4: Low Achievers and Social Media

A colleague spent a year working with lower achievers who were also categorized as emotionally disturbed teenagers. He began to find that he was the subject of false accusations online, was illegally recorded by students in class, and was being set up by students and parents in an effort to oust him from the school. Fake social media accounts and doctored photos appeared to show the teacher in morally compromising positions with parents and students.

The school district did very little to support the teacher overtly. The student was disciplined for targeting the teacher. But the school could not do much because most of the assault against the teacher was done from home.

The teacher threatened to sue the student and his family, but the student and family resorted to the excuse that *it was only a joke and everyone does this sort of thing now*. The teacher was subsequently given a different teaching assignment and went on with his career. To this day, the teacher in question carries psychological scars from the prolonged assault on his reputation and character. Teachers must be able to defend against such false allegations.[33]

Anecdote #5: The High School Principal

A local high school principal had been accused of verbally and emotionally abusing his staff while running a school by bullying and shaming. The administrative staff demanded obedience and made periodic threats to faculty who did not perform as expected, making the working environment hostile and unsavory for teachers.

The principal was investigated and found to be abusive. He was ultimately demoted from his administrative position and placed back into the class-

room as an instructor.[34] In a complete housecleaning, the school's entire administrative staff was also dismissed and reassigned.

Stories like these abound. Every community has these types of anecdotes. The saddest part is that many of these conflicts occur and no one reports them. There are many reasons for the lack of reporting. Sometimes, it is fear and reprisal. Other times, reports are not filed so as not to appear weak. Whatever the case, whether being too busy or too inexperienced in the profession—or even near the end of a career—unless these issues are reported, school districts and families operate under the notion that all is well between the walls and down the halls of their children's schools. Clearly, change is required.

A NATIONAL SURVEY OF EDUCATORS

The point has already been established that each year, education professionals claim to be victimized by a range of assaults against their person, property, and reputation. Educators claim this victimization through a range of threats, including verbal, physical, and sexual assaults[35] as well as property damage and online damage to their reputations. These assaults are wide ranging, beginning in the primary grades and continuing through college.

Public and private colleges are also seeing an increase in assaults upon professors, ranging from getting them fired for beliefs that do not match a certain segment of the student population or ruining the reputations of professors through social media and protest to outright physical beatings. Nearly 20.5 million college students were enrolled in 2016, which is 5 million more than were enrolled in 2000. Professors have come across some changing attitudes on college campuses, and not all of these changes are for the better,[36] which sometimes results in backlash or even worse.

The purpose of the survey taken was for research for this book. The gathering of data was specific to educators' experiences at their schools. The media reports of teachers' being assaulted became quite alarming over the past few years. Therefore, the survey was an attempt to discover whether the problems of teacher assault were as extensive as they appeared in the literature.

Construction of the Survey

To begin, the survey was constructed to gain understanding about assaults upon educational professionals in general. The first category of the survey was given the title General Background, where demographic information was requested. The rest of the survey categories included specific questions pertaining to educators' experiences with assaults.

Each of seven additional survey sections requested information pertaining to assaults coinciding with (1) assaults in general, (2) threats at work, (3) online threats and bullying, (4) verbal assaults, (5) physical assaults, (6) sexual assaults, and (7) personal property damage.

Survey Distribution

The data were requested anonymously and compiled over a period of three weeks. The website used for the data collection was Survey Monkey, and the analysis of the data was done in Excel. For ease of reporting, rounding of numbers by Excel should be assumed, without significantly or statistically altering the conclusions or analysis of the results.

The link to the survey was posted on social media sites, such as Facebook, Twitter, and Reddit. The link was also posted on school district web pages; college, university, and public school teacher faculty association web pages in large school districts; the National Education Association and American Federation of Teachers websites; and on select state departments of education web pages. Educators were allowed to share the survey with colleagues within their local spheres. In sum, over the course of twenty days, there were 435 respondents, who spent an average of 4 minutes and 42 seconds each as they took a forty-five-question survey.

Data Collection

The data were collected from many states, with even a few international responses. The international responses are not included in the data analysis. However, it became clear from the responses that the problem of teacher assaults is not exclusive to the United States. The highlights of the data are summarized in bullet points below, categorized by the way they appear in the survey. Some of the more salient and interesting results are included in the summary.

HIGHLIGHTS OF THE NATIONAL SURVEY

1. Demographics (Questions 1–9)

- The distribution of years of experience in education was quite even across three of the four categories, with teachers in the 11–20-year range topping the list at 36 percent.
- The age ranges of teacher respondents consisted of the following: 41–50-year-old teachers responding at 30 percent and 21–30 and 51–60 each reporting at 16 percent.
- Eighty-one percent were female.

- Seventy-one percent were classroom teachers.
- The top seven respondent states are listed in Table 1.1.

Table 1.1. Top Seven Respondent States

States	Number of Surveys Submitted	Percentage of Survey Respondents
California	170	39%
New York	22	5%
Florida	20	5%
New Jersey	20	5%
Washington	18	4%
Texas	14	3%
Tennessee	10	2%
TOTAL	274	63%
All Others	*161*	*37%*

- Eighty-four percent work in public schools.
- Twenty-eight percent are employed in public secondary schools (grades 9–12), and 27 percent are employed in primary level public education (grades K–3). Intermediate respondents (grades 4–6) were 17 percent, and junior high/middle school respondents were 13 percent.
- Eighty-nine percent do not work exclusively with special education students.
- Ninety percent indicated they had special needs students in their classrooms.

2. Assaults: General (Questions 10–15)

- Forty-four percent responded they had definitely been assaulted while employed as teachers.
- Forty percent responded they had never been assaulted while employed as teachers.
- Fifty percent responded that in the past one to three years they would not consider an assault of any type to have been committed against them while at work. Twenty-six percent indicated they had been assaulted one or two times in the past one to three years while at work.
- Teachers who had been assaulted at work responded that 57 percent of the time their superiors were informed about the assaults.
- Fifty-one percent of the assaults reported by the teachers to their superiors did not result in a police report. Only 5 percent of the respondents indicated their superiors filed police reports about the assault.

- Fourteen percent of those assaulted at work had to be treated medically for their injuries. Forty-eight percent of those assaulted at work did not receive any official medical care.
- Twenty-four percent of those assaulted at work indicated they were satisfied with the way the incidents were handled by administrators. Thirty-five percent of those assaulted were not satisfied with the way the incidents were handled.

3. Assaults: Threats at Work (Questions 16–19)

- Fifty-five percent indicated they had been approached in a threatening manner by parents while at work.
- Twenty-six percent indicated they had been approached by a colleague in a threatening manner while at work. Seventy-three percent responded they had not been approached in a threatening manner by a colleague while at work.
- Twenty-seven percent responded they had been approached by an administrator in a threatening manner. Seventy-two percent indicated they had not been approached by an administrator in a threatening manner.
- Sixty-four percent had been approached by one or more students in a threatening manner while at work.

4. Assaults: Online Threats and Bullying (Questions 20–24)

- Twenty-three percent indicated they had been bullied online because of their actions in education. Seventy-four percent said they had not been bullied online because of their actions in education.
- Eight percent responded they had been bullied on social media sites by a colleague. Ninety-one percent said they had not been bullied on social media by a colleague.
- Ninety-six percent indicated they had not been bullied on social media by an administrator.
- Twenty-percent indicated they had been bullied online through social media posting by a parent of one of their students. Seventy-nine percent responded they had not been the subject of social media bullying online.
- Twelve percent responded they had been the subject of students' social media bullying online. Eighty-six percent indicated they had not been the subject of students' social media bullying online.

5. Assaults: Verbal (Questions 25–30)

- Twenty-one percent indicated they had been verbally assaulted directly because of their gender. Seventy-seven percent indicated they had not been verbally assaulted directly because of their gender.
- Sixty-four percent indicated they had been verbally assaulted by one or more students.
- Twenty-nine percent indicated they had been verbally assaulted by one or more of their administrators. Seventy percent indicated they had not been verbally assaulted by one or more of their administrators.
- Forty-three percent indicated they had been verbally assaulted by a parent while they were working. Five percent indicated they had been verbally assaulted after work.
- Nine percent of the teachers who also coached indicated they had been verbally assaulted by a parent.

6. Assaults: Physical (Questions 31–36)

- Twenty-four percent indicated they had been purposefully spit at or on by one or more students. Sixty-six percent indicated they had not been spit at or on.
- Thirty-four percent indicated they had been purposefully kicked by one or more students. Sixty-one percent indicated they had not been purposefully kicked by one or more students.
- Forty-six percent responded they had had objects thrown at them by one or more students. Fifty percent responded they had not had objects thrown at them by one or more students.
- Forty-one percent indicated they had been physically assaulted by one or more students using their hands. Fifty-three percent indicated they had not been physically assaulted by one or more students using their hands.
- Ninety-six percent indicated they had not been physically assaulted by a colleague while at work.
- Two percent indicated they had been physically assaulted by a parent.

7. Assaults: Sexual (Questions 37–40)

- Eight percent responded they had experienced sexual advances or sexual pressure from one or more students. Fifty-six percent indicated they had not experienced sexual advances or sexual pressure from one or more students.
- Nine percent indicated they had experienced sexual advances or sexual pressure from a colleague. Eighty-four percent indicated they had not experienced sexual advances or sexual pressure from a colleague.

- Ninety-four percent indicated they had not experienced sexual advances or sexual pressure from an administrator. One percent indicated they had experienced sexual advances or sexual pressure from an administrator.
- Eighty-eight percent responded they had not experienced sexual advances or sexual pressure from a parent. Six percent indicated they had experienced sexual advances or sexual pressure from a parent.

8. Assaults: Personal Property Damage (Questions 41–44)

- Sixty-one percent indicated their personal property had been damaged by students while at work. Thirty-three percent indicated that personal property had not been damaged by students while at work.
- Ninety-two percent indicated they did not have their personal property damaged by a parent while at work.
- Six percent indicated they experienced personal property damage by students while away from work and at home.
- Zero percent indicated that their personal property was damaged while away from work and at home.

9. Additional Written-In Anecdotes

(This list is abbreviated. An extensive list appears in Appendix 1; this list comprises only written-in responses to question 45.)

- "Student offered sexual favors for a better grade."
- "Educators have no rights and are subjected to so very much."
- "My iPhone was stolen at work. I know who took it, and he knows I know. But nothing was done."
- "I know several teachers who have been verbally attacked or physically attacked by students."
- "The students who were assaulting me were assaulting others, including students. I was bothered that I could not provide a safe environment for my students."
- "I have had colleagues cyberbullied online by students through social media and by tagging at our school."
- "My district has a restraining order against a parent due to verbal abuse and threatened physical assault."
- "I know of administrators cursing up storms and yelling at teachers at the tops of their voices while their office doors are closed."
- "Once a student threatened to smoke me. He was removed from the classroom but continued to harass me."

WHAT NEEDS TO BE DONE

In 2013, the American Psychological Association and the National Education Association joined forces to study a problem that had not received as much attention as it should have received. The organizations set up a group and gave the group the title "Violence Against Teachers Task Force." The study collected teacher-reported incidents, a national survey on teacher victimization, and additional case studies.

According to the study abstract, "Violence directed toward teachers has been understudied, despite significant media and empirical investigation on school violence."[37] If these conclusions are valid, and there is no reason to doubt that they are, then the problem of violence against teachers is much worse than imagined.

Additional studies need to be undertaken. There is no doubt there are causes and effects related to teachers' assaults. However, the assumption should be made that a vast number of assaults against teachers are not being reported, for an assortment of reasons. Any effort to reconcile the record of reporting is likely to be met with apprehension by a school district. What is needed is transparency.

The politically correct social justice and restorative justice programs are weighted more heavily in their favor than any programs of protection for teachers. Regardless of the reporting issue, schools must do more to include programs that balance safety and support for teachers wishing to officially report violence on campuses.

Schools should be about producing excellent citizens. Likewise, education should about changing lives or strengthening families, not weakening them and replacing them. Violent tendencies expressed by students have to be controlled, shaped, or changed from within to move the needle of safety in a positive direction. A student has to want to change and behave. No program can change human nature. Therefore, the question at this juncture about such change is how best to reach the *effect* of the students toward taking ownership of change.

Three good beginning steps that serve toward understanding and dealing with the problems addressed throughout this chapter include *revisitation*, *reexamination*, and *engagement*.

Step 1: Revisiting and reworking "after-the-fact" programs that do not hold students accountable after they have committed an assault upon a teacher must be reformed. Progressive policies that place students at the center of the education universe, but lessen accountability for actions, are failing across the nation. Student centrism has produced little monarchs.

Step 2: Reexamination of political policies must occur. Any policy based on profiling of students while assuming that any lack of such policy results in a school-to-prison pipeline is specious. Students who commit crimes are clearly placing themselves in the pipeline already.

What are the schools' responsibilities to make certain students do not assault others? An act of assault is a serious crime. Communities and schools must band together to support each other and ensure that rearing and educating children and students are done by more than programs. Partnering with families is essential and a step in the right direction.

Step 3: Engaging families in deeper support of the local schools and committing to working together on behalf of educating children will foster a new environment. This is the essence of successful education of any student. Families and their involvement are the keys to ultimate and lasting success. Unfortunately, the relationships between schools, teachers, students, and families are strained today. The rebuilding of positive relationships between these stakeholders should be of primary and critical importance.

Violence against teachers is a serious problem in today's American public education. But it exists in all schools, including schools from other nations. Is it merely human nature to be violent? Can culture be reshaped toward safety and recapture basic expressions of consideration, courtesy, and politeness? Without consequences for behaviors, there is little chance of recapturing any semblance of a previous cultural paradigm.

NOTES

1. Richard Worzel. "Why parents don't respect teachers." *Teach Magazine.* October 12, 2017. Retrieved from www.teachmag.com/archives/128.

2. Catherine M. Wilson, Kevin S. Douglas, and David R. Lyon. "Violence against teachers: Prevalence and consequences." *Journal of Interpersonal Violence.* October 1, 2010. Retrieved from www.ncbi.nlm.nih.gov/pubmed/20889535.

3. "Violence." *Merriam Webster Dictionary.* Retrieved from www.merriam-webster.com/dictionary/violence.

4. Samantha Schmidt. "After months of bullying, her parents say, a 12-year-old New Jersey girl killed herself. They blame the school." *The Washington Post.* August 4, 2017. Retrieved from www.washingtonpost.com/news/morning-mix/wp/2017/08/02/after-months-of-bullying-a-12-year-old-new-jersey-girl-killed-herself-her-parents-blame-the-school/?utm_term=.28304ea08edf. CF. Staff. "Girl, 13, commits suicide after being cyber-bullied by neighbor posing as teenage boy." *Daily Mail.* November 19, 2007. Retrieved from www.dailymail.co.uk/news/article-494809/Girl-13-commits-suicide-cyber-bullied-neighbour-posing-teenage-boy.html.

5. Jina Yoon, Michael L. Sulkowski, and Sheri A. Bauman. "Teachers' responses to bullying incidents: Effects of teacher characteristics and contexts." October 27, 2014. *Journal of School Violence.* Vol. 15, No. 1. Retrieved from www.tandfonline.com/doi/abs/10.1080/15388220.2014.963592?journalCode=wjsv20.

6. Ernest J. Zarra III. *Teacher-Student Relationships: Crossing into the Emotional, Physical, and Sexual Realms.* 2013. Lanham, MD: Rowman & Littlefield.

7. Staff. "Student arrested after classroom attack on NJ high school teacher caught on video." *FOXNEWS.* January 27, 2015. Retrieved from www.foxnews.com/us/2015/01/27/student-arrested-after-classroom-attack-on-nj-high-school-teacher-caught-on.html.

8. Neil Munro. "Obama backs race-based school discipline policies." *The Daily Caller*. July 2, 2012. Retrieved from http://dailycaller.com/2012/07/27/obama-backs-race-based-school-discipline-policies/.

9. Staff. "Lawmakers ask DeVos not to repeal disciplinary protections for minority students." *CBS-19 NewsPlex*. December 18, 2017. Retrieved from www.newsplex.com/content/news/Lawmakers-ask-DeVos-not-to-repeal-disciplinary-protections-for-minority-students-465020883.html.

10. Ibid.

11. Blake Neff. "Teachers strongly oppose Obama effort to regulate suspensions." *The Daily Caller*. August 18, 2015. Retrieved from http://dailycaller.com/2015/08/18/teachers-strongly-oppose-obama-effort-to-regulate-suspensions/.

12. Susan Du. "Johnson teacher is sucker punched from behind while breaking up fight." *City Pages*. March 15, 2016. Retrieved from www.citypages.com/news/johnson-teacher-is-sucker-punched-from-behind-while-breaking-up-fight-8123227.

13. Wilborn P. Nobles III. "Black students 2 times as likely to be suspended as white peers, Tulane study says." *The Times-Picayune*. November 21, 2017. Retrieved from www.nola.com/education/index.ssf/2017/11/student_discipline_racial_gaps.html.

14. Ibid.

15. Du, "Johnson teacher is sucker punched from behind while breaking up fight."

16. Erin Hinrichs. "Whatever happened to time-outs? Minneapolis and St. Paul districts still suspend hundreds of elementary students each year." *MinnPost*. October 19, 2017. Retrieved from www.minnpost.com/education/2017/10/whatever-happened-time-outs-minneapolis-and-st-paul-districts-still-suspend-hundre.

17. Ibid.

18. Staff. "Student charged with assault after fighting high school teacher." *NBC4*. September 21, 2016. Retrieved from http://nbc4i.com/2016/09/21/student-charged-with-assault-after-fighting-high-school-teacher/.

19. Ibid.

20. Staff. "Kindergartners behind latest incidents at unruly Woodland Hills school." *WTAE-TV*. November 13, 2015. Retrieved from http://www.wtae.com/article/kindergartners-behind-latest-incidents-at-unruly-woodland-hills-school/7475144.

21. Ibid.

22. Ibid.

23. Sara Satullo. "Allentown teachers get higher pay, assault protections in new pact." *Lehigh Valley Live*. March 15, 2016. Retrieved from www.lehighvalleylive.com/allentown/index.ssf/2016/03/allentown_teachers_to_see_high.html.

24. Ibid.

25. Ibid.

26. Will Flanders and Natalie Goodnow. "Obama school discipline policies hurt Wisconsin kids." *Journal Sentinel*. November 27, 2017. Retrieved from www.jsonline.com/story/opinion/contributors/2017/11/27/obama-school-discipline-policies-hurt-wisconsin-kids/888583001/.

27. Noel K. Gallagher. "Maine teachers say new restraint rule leads to assaults by students." *Portland Press Herald*. November 26, 2012. Retrieved from www.centralmaine.com/2012/11/26/maine-teachers-union-reports-dozens-of-student-on-teacher-assaults/.

28. Ibid.

29. Ibid.

30. Ibid.

31. Sherry Posnick-Goodwin. "Budget cuts exacerbate safety concerns." June 11, 2011. *California Educator*, p. 19.

32. California's Public School Accountability Act of 1999. "Academic Performance Index." *California Department of Education*. Retrieved from www.cde.ca.gov/ta/ac/ap/.

33. Thomas Milton Stern. "Defending against student assault claims." *North Carolina Association of Educators*. Retrieved from www.ncae.org/wp-content/uploads/Defending-against-student-assault.pdf.

34. Kyle Harvey. "Evidence uncovered in firing of Mira Monte HS principal." *Bakersfield Now*. June 10, 2015. Retrieved from http://bakersfieldnow.com/news/local/evidence-uncovered-in-firing-of-mira-monte-hs-principal.

35. Katie Mulvaney. "Former student accused of sexually assaulting teacher." *Providence Journal*. September 29, 2017. Retrieved from http://www.providencejournal.com/news/20170929/former-student-accused-of-sexually-assaulting-teacher.

36. Greg Lukianoff and Jonathan Haidt. "The coddling of the American mind: How trigger warnings are hurting mental health on campus." *The Atlantic*. September 2015. Retrieved from www.theatlantic.com/magazine/archive/2015/09/the-coddling-of-the-american-mind/399356/.

37. Linda A. Reddy, Dorothy Espelage, Susan D. McMahon, et al. 2013. "Violence against teachers: Case studies from the APA Task Force." *International Journal of School & Educational Psychology*. Vol. 1, No. 4, pp. 231–245.

Chapter Two

The Extent of the Problem

> I am no longer safe at my workplace. I cannot continue to work in a place that
> is so unhealthy and dangerous. I also cannot watch my students and colleagues
> suffer in this environment any longer.
> —Kersten Wescott's letter of resignation, Green Bay School District [1]

Violence against teachers is viewed by the American Psychological Association (APA) as "a silent national crisis." In the 2011 study published by the APA's Task Force, the conclusion is drawn that "Violence directed against K–12 teachers is a serious problem that demands the immediate attention of researchers, school administrators, community leaders and policymakers."[2] Additionally, just before the rise of Generation Z and its first graduates from college (2015), the 2011–2012 school years[3] saw terrific rises in violence against teachers.[4] For example:

- Eighty percent of teachers reported at least one victimization experience in the current or the previous year of the survey.
- Ninety-four percent claimed to have been victimized by students.
- Nearly 50 percent of the teachers claimed they had been victimized by two or more different types of perpetrators.
- At least one incident of being harassed was reported by 72.5 percent.
- Fifty percent of the teachers experienced property damage.
- Forty-four percent reported physical attacks.

In 2015, the Institute of Education Sciences (IES), in conjunction with the U.S. Department of Justice and the National Center for Education Statistics, published the official report of a 2014 study on School Crime and Safety (see Table 2.1).[5] However, there were several factors mitigating the accuracy of the percentages reported on violence against teachers.

Some of these factors include the following: (1) Millions of students are no longer in public schools, opting for homeschooling and private schooling. (2) There is no certainty that all violent actions that occur toward teachers from K–12 are reported. Some are underreported, making the number appear to be improving[6] or just not reported at all.[7] In fact, (3) there is clear evidence that teachers of special needs and special education students, as well as those in the younger primary grades, are the group that experiences daily bumps and bruises from violent students, yet these go unreported officially due to state law or district policy.[8]

SERIOUS PROBLEMS IN AMERICAN PUBLIC SCHOOLS

Four serious problems exist in American public schools. These problems are in the way of academics and student achievement. The first and foremost concern that affects education on a grand scale in the United States is the breakdown of the family. As the family goes, so too goes culture. Culture comes into each classroom in America every moment of every day, and so do family concerns.

A second problem is drug and alcohol abuse. Addictions are on the rise, and the opioid crisis is beyond epidemic proportions. In fact, it is worse than anyone had imagined.[9] More and more students are coming to school with residual effects from home lives affected by drugs and alcohol. Also, first-hand and secondhand smoke from marijuana is also leaving students in stupors,[10] and these effects are visible as far down as the elementary level.

A third problem affecting education is the number of inappropriate relationships that teachers are having with students. These relationships have become deeply emotional, highly physical, and overtly sexual. Teachers are being arrested in record numbers for inappropriate and illegal relationships with students as early as elementary school. Along with the arrests of teachers, students are also arrested when there are extenuating circumstances, such as blackmail, social media bullying, or threats.

A fourth serious problem in American public schools is violence. Violence between students is not only increasing and dangerous, but it can also be deadly. Students and parents are assaulting teachers and coaches and posting their *anger videos* and comments on social media sites. Violence against teachers, including verbal and physical assaults, has been on the rise, both in the classrooms and deep within social media platforms on the Internet.

Table 2.1. State List of Reported Assaults against Teachers

State	# of Public and Charter School Teachers during 2011–2012	% of Public and Charter School Teachers Reporting *Threats* during 2011–2012	% of Public and Charter School Teachers Reporting *Physical Attacks* during 2011–2012	State	# of Public and Charter School Teachers during 2011–2012	% of Public and Charter School Teachers Reporting *Threats* during 2011–2012	% of Public and Charter School Teachers Reporting *Physical Attacks* during 2011–2012
AL	45,000	7.6	3.1	MT	12,400	7.6	4.2
AK	7,500	12.3	5.1	NE	23,900	8.0	5.8
AZ	61,700	9.1	4.7	NV	25,200	9.1	4.7
AR	37,700	7.8	5.2	NH	15,700	5.6	NR
CA	285,500	7.7	4.4	NJ	125,200	6.9	3.6
CO	55,900	7.3	3.6	NM	21,700	10.0	9.9
CT	44,900	7.5	6.2	NY	241,400	11.9	7.0
DE	9,300	15.8	9.8	NC	104,300	13.4	6.3
DC	NR	NR	NR	ND	10,300	6.1	3.3
FL	NR	NR	NR	OH	122,100	9.9	3.9
GA	123,300	9.5	6.3	OK	46,200	9.6	6.2
HI	NR	NR	NR	OR	31,800	5.3	3.4
ID	16,300	6.7	3.6	PA	148,800	10.1	4.4
IL	140,900	7.3	4.1	RI	NR	NR	NR
IN	64,000	11.2	6.4	SC	51,800	13.1	NR

	Number of Teachers		
IA	36,100	11.7	7.6
KS	36,500	7.2	5.5
KY	46,800	10.6	7.0
LA	44,500	18.3	7.2
ME	18,400	9.1	5.2
MD	NR	NR	NR
MA	79,200	6.2	5.3
MI	96,700	11.8	9.0
MN	62,300	11.4	6.5
MS	37,600	7.7	3.1
MO	68,700	12.3	7.5
SD	10,800	10.0	5.2
TN	76,500	9.4	3.2
TX	350,800	10.0	5.7
UT	27,900	7.2	5.4
VT	9,400	8.7	5.3
VA	88,500	9.9	6.5
WA	55,500	7.4	6.8
WV	24,200	9.4	4.3
WI	66,800	13.7	11.3
WY	8,500	10.9	NR

Total Number of Teachers 2011–2012: 3,385,200

National Averages: (1) Reported Threats: 10.0%; (2) Reported Attacks: 5.8%

School Crime

According to the *Indicators of School Crime and Safety Report of 2014* (ISCS), which is a comprehensive report of representative samples and universe surveys on crime in American schools, "Our nation's schools should be safe havens for teaching and learning, free of crime and violence. Any instance of crime or violence at school not only affects the individuals involved, but also may disrupt the educational process and affect bystanders, the school itself, and the surrounding community."[11]

Public schools are not isolated in reporting problems between students, students toward property, and violence against teachers. The ISCS validates this point in its report, publishing data from ten sources. Five of these sources include:

1. *Campus Safety and Security Survey* (2001–2012)
2. *EDFacts* (2008–2009 and 2012–2013)
3. *School Crime Supplement to the National Crime Victimization Survey* (1995, 1999, and 2001–2013 biennially)
4. *School Survey on Crime and Safety* (1999–2000 and 2003–2010)
5. *Schools and Staffing Survey* (1993–1994, 1999–2000, 2003–2004, 2007–2008, and 2011–2012)

The data are clear. Some of the key findings presented in the ISCS include:

- There were reported forty-five school-associated violent deaths in one school calendar year (July 1, 2011, through June 30, 2012).
- In 2013, in the student age range of 12–18, there were an estimated 1.5 million nonfatal victimizations at school.
- Of the 1.5 million nonfatal victimizations, there were about 500,000 thefts and 1 million violent victimizations.

The conclusions drawn from the data are very interesting. Students are not the *only* victims of intimidation and violence at schools. Teachers are also subject to threats and physical attacks, and students from their schools are now on official record as committing these offenses. However, as already mentioned, large numbers of assaults go unreported officially each year.

Another survey, the Schools and Staffing Survey (SASS), asked school teachers whether they were threatened with injury or physically attacked by a student from their school in the previous twelve months. "During the 2011–12 school year, 9 percent of school teachers were threatened with injury by a student from their school. . . . The percentage of teachers reporting they had been physically attacked by a student from their school in

2011–12 (5 percent) was higher than in any previous year (ranging from 3 to 4 percent).[12]

VIOLENCE IN SCHOOLS IS A PANDEMIC

To begin, the United States and other nations must take the issue of violence in schools more seriously. "Violence directed toward teachers has been understudied, and has received limited media and policy attention in the United States and internationally."[13]

In the United Kingdom, one of the concerns about violence against teachers being understudied is because it is underreported. Academies and schools that are outside the state purview are not required to report their assaults. In Bristol, England, incidents of reported abuse included "being hit, kicked, sworn at and sexually assaulted."[14]

The National Union of Teachers took a survey of three thousand members in Bristol, England. They discovered in the self-reporting that "more than 70 percent had been victims of physical attacks, sexual assaults or verbal abuse."[15] Some teachers report the assaults, but others sense it is a general "waste of time to report."[16] This same attitude of indifference exists in the United States.

The majority of "psychological definitions and studies of school violence acknowledge that violent acts occur within social contexts (i.e., classrooms, schools, neighborhoods, social media) and involve complex social interactions between and among individuals; however, educators are often overlooked as victims."[17] The end result is that "the reality of violence directed against educators is an unfortunate occurrence for many who work in education systems. Such violence ranges from disrespectful behavior to bullying or intimidation, verbal threats or gestures, theft, property damage, and in some cases, physical assault."[18]

Violence directed at teachers is an international crisis. However, despite this *reporting reality*, the violence itself "is rarely defined, empirically studied, or meaningfully discussed within academic circles."[19] For example, in Wales, United Kingdom, the Welsh government reported that "the number of assaults average at eight per school day . . . (of which) 1,268 were physical and 77 verbal"[20] for a three-year period. In the Cymru district, the teachers' union has stated the assaults "not only had an impact on individual teachers but disrupted the classroom environment"[21] and outside the classroom with parents assaulting teachers.[22]

TRENDS OF VIOLENCE

Whether it is Wales, England, Australia, Ireland, China, the United States—or anywhere else—teachers are being assaulted in growing numbers. The continents of Asia and Africa[23] are experiencing increases in abusive behaviors and violence toward teachers.

Also, in Scotland, "more than £290,000 in compensation has been paid to Scottish teachers and lecturers over the past year following assaults and other injuries at work."[24] The Educational Institute of Scotland (EIS) has stated that "teachers and lecturers are entitled to safe workplaces and the evidence . . . is a worrying testimony to a lack of diligence by employers."[25]

Again, to reiterate, the United States is not alone in having to figure out what to do with students who are becoming increasingly more violent toward teachers. Violence in schools has become a very serious international problem as well.

Germany

In a ten-year span, from 1999–2009, "more than 20 teachers of German schools died as a result of attacks."[26] Attacks have occurred based on ethnicity, anger about grades, religion, and sexual orientation and expression as well as mere cruelty. According to the Forsa Institute for Social Research, 59 percent of teachers surveyed claimed to have been victims of student violence. The study also revealed that there is an alarming growth of teachers being violently victimized both physically and mentally by students.[27]

China

In China, for instance, teachers and students sometimes become involved in fights in the classroom. Internal investigations handle the fallout and repercussions. For example, in April 2016, at a Fanji High School in Mengcheng County, Anhui, China, an in-class melee broke out for about a minute between a teacher of English and several high school boys. It was captured on video.

The video shows Mr. Ma "attempting to take a piece of paper from a student, who refuses to hand it over."[28] Within the course of a few seconds, the "teacher then appears to put his hand to the teenager's throat. The student hits Ma in retaliation and pushes him into a corner."[29]

A few seconds later, "several more boys rush in and start punching and kicking the teacher, who fights back and slaps one of his assailants in the face."[30] Things appear to settle down, and the class apparently resumes. Former students of Ma have called him a very professional teacher. The local police were assigned to investigate the case.[31]

Another example, one with a more tragic outcome, involves a teacher in China who had confiscated a student's phone. A Chinese student "slit the throat"[32] of his chemistry teacher a day after his cell phone was confiscated by the instructor. The student, named Lei, "had been discovered playing with his phone by his teacher Sun Wakang during a chemistry lesson at a school in in Fuzhou, eastern China's Jiangxi Province. The following day Lei went to Mr. Sun's classroom where the teacher was . . . marking papers, and slit his throat from behind.

"The 32-year-old father-of-one died at the scene as the student fled. The student eventually called the local emergency number and confessed to the crime before turning himself in to police in Shanghai."[33]

Australia

In 2016, a 15-year-old boy was arrested in Australia for assaulting a teacher after he shoved and punched the instructor in the face, causing the need for medical attention. The union president representing the school stated that "the union was aware of a number of instances . . . involving violent student behavior at the school."[34] The school name could not be released to the general public for legal reasons, according to policy.

Circumstances escalated emotions at the school and forced the education department in the region to post "security guards at the school . . . after a brawl between students and parents erupted in the school carpark."[35] In referring to teacher assaults and parent incidents, the State School Teachers Union president, Pat Byrne, indicated that "these types of violent incidents were symptomatic of issues outside the school."[36]

Australia has been dealing with teacher assaults for some time. According to Education Department figures, approximately five Australian teachers are assaulted each day. These are just the officially reported assaults. In 2012 alone, figures showed "there were 1,062 assaults on teachers in the states' public system—an average of more than five every school day."[37]

Canada

In Winnipeg, Canada, "dozens of school staff, including teachers, have been assaulted"[38] in the past few years. Exact numbers are difficult to ascertain, as with most school districts around the globe. "The Manitoba Teachers' Society says that actual number of assaults on teachers is higher than the numbers show, because administrators discourage teachers from reporting incidents and some incidents do not lead to suspension."

This has now become a typical outcome at many schools.[39] In the Winnipeg School Division, the major problem for physical violence outbreak is drugs.[40] This leads to the question of how many assaults of teachers are carried out with students who are intoxicated, or "high," on illegal substances? Do districts ever examine or care to discover the answer to this question?

TEACHERS UNDER DURESS

The APA Task Force on Violence Against Teachers accumulated several case studies that illustrate the nature of the stressors facing teachers and highlight the increase of these stressors throughout the course of their workdays and at home. Each case study is summarized, and actions that were taken are included as well.

The results of the case studies are quite revealing. Collectively, teachers reported "experiencing violence from students, parents, and colleagues, suggesting that students are not the only individuals that need to be included in violence directed toward teacher prevention efforts. Furthermore, violence is not limited to the school hours; teachers report being targeted at home and through the Internet."[41]

As the Internet and social media proliferate in popularity and usage in America's teenagers' and young adults' daily regimens, its popularity is being used to "perpetuate aggression and violence among students. . . . [I]t is not surprising that teachers are being targeted through technology."[42]

RELUCTANT TEACHERS

Teachers are not usually a high-profile bunch. Most are swamped with the daily requirements of working with students. In fact, the energies that could be put to use to create and innovate for the larger context of education as a whole are being used more and more on nonteaching tasks. The energy to step up and be heard on issues if it means sacrificing time in class or that paperwork would pile up in the process is limited to more urgent issues.

Teachers are as reluctant to take the lead as they are fatigued and seek to avoid undertaking one additional task for work. There is also a large segment of newer and midcareer teachers fearful of administrative retribution for speaking out about issues, particularly if they are probationary, pretenured, temporary, noncredentialed, or simply in need of the job for the sake of economics.

All teachers fear being labeled as incompetent or weak to their administrators. A small number of teachers hope to rise into the administrative ranks and avoid anything that smacks of controversy. As a result, teachers of all stripes keep their heads down and make it through each day the best they can.

FEAR OF ACTION

Politicians and bureaucrats are unenthusiastic in calling for arrests of students who act out violently and are more inclined to make excuses for their behaviors. They even pass laws to give credence to their excuses for behaviors. Anything to the contrary would affect some of their constituent groups' political support.

In some states, the teachers' unions are some of the largest supporters of politicians, especially Democrats. However, racial and ethnic civil rights groups also tend to be Democrats, which sets up some conflicts of interest for politicians. Any policy that supports teachers, yet is somewhat responsible for the rise of discipline issues with the very groups protected by the policy, places constituents at odds with each other. How is this good for either side?

A litigious society is highly restrictive—even in the face of doing what is right. Most school psychologists and intervention strategy experts are in the same camp. Combining the two means school personnel are cautioned to take care to understand there is always triggering or driving students to act in the extreme. The message is to avoid lawsuits at all *cost.*

So in efforts to reclassify student behaviors, behavioral psychologists inform a new generation of teachers that human behavior is *caused.* The student himself or herself is not completely to blame. Someone or something else is to be blamed, possibly illustrating that the student is a victim of his or her own positioning as center of the education universe. [43]

Inexperience Speaks Volumes

One criticism levied upon school psychologists is their limited time spent in the classroom. Education professionals who spent significant time in the classroom trenches before rising in their specialty careers are much more respected by teachers. Lacking significant classroom time means that working directly with students in emerging generations also is lacking.

Today's students are very different than those of a decade ago. However, in their defense, psychologists, like others with caseloads at schools, are so overburdened and *snowed under* with paperwork that they do not always have the time to spend in classrooms to observe the problems for which they offer solutions. If teachers used these reasons for not managing their classrooms, they would be evaluated poorly. Many teachers are overwhelmed with programs and are still drowning in assessments, yet each teacher is expected to accomplish things akin to daily miracles.

The uniqueness of schools sometimes means that disciplinary measures are often handled differently, even with the same distributive disciplinary policy in hand. For example, finding "reasons" as to why a student hits a teacher in the nose with his or her fist is very important.

Sometimes, incidents such as these are considered accidental or part of the expectations when working with students who may be emotionally or mentally disturbed. Severely disabled students are sometimes very violent, but there is always the question as to whether they understand any of their actions. However, sometimes a student is just mean-spirited and decides to act on his or her natural inclination at the moment, special needs or not.

In the main, exploring students' reasons for actions should not be of primary concern if consequences are not explored equally. The issue is what are the consequences so that the student can learning from the error in judgment or error in action. Without correction, how long might it be before one such student grows up and is held accountable for something much more deeply contrived or expressed?[44]

Ask any group of veteran teachers of a decade or more experience, and they can usually refer back in time to former students whom they identified as exhibiting precursors to behaviors for serious future violent actions. Today, the flagrant actions and assaults by students are greater in number, and it makes no difference what the students' race or background is.

Teachers in lower grades are experiencing precursors to future violence firsthand. Some of the stories from elementary schools are frightening. Yet teachers are expected to work with these students, putting themselves at greater risk in the process. (See chapter 4 for additional discussion on these matters.)

Teachers are expected to perform wonders in the face of less respect from parents and students and lessened support from administrators. Take for example one of the many risk factors for teachers today: the bipolar student. This student "can experience great irritability, building to a rage if not recognized and dealt with in an appropriate and timely manner."[45] Managing students such as these is way above the self-professed pay grade of the average teacher.

MINIMIZING VIOLENCE

Instead of calling out students' actions for being violent, the actions are too often classified as accidents or incidents. This tends to minimize the assaults. Sometimes, the teachers themselves minimize these incidents and label them as accidental. Other times, the administrators pressure teachers to classify assaults as accidents.

There are enough data available to conclude that administrators place blame for some of the student outbursts on less-than-desirable teacher classroom management. Consequently, that fear is one reason teachers tend to minimize the violence directed at them. No doubt some pretty bad teachers can be found in some schools. But when it comes to violence, even involving bad teachers, a serious line must be drawn.

As terrible as that seems, students are often allowed to return to school or even to the same class in a short period of time after an incident of assault upon a teacher. Such a response to a student's violent actions is irresponsible and minimizes the violence. Parents entrust their children to the care of the school and expect safety for them.

All persons involved in witnessing a student's violent outburst are affected. Brisk administrative responses of sending students back into classrooms infuriate teachers and place everyone on alert for their next violent outburst. This cannot be a decent and secure learning environment. It is certainly not a safer one for teachers.

What is often communicated by dismissing student behavior is that the issue is not as serious as the teacher had made it out to be. Are bureaucrats really this disengaged? If an administrator had violent students in his or her office multiple hours per day and these students swore at the administrators, threw objects at them and their office staff, or punched the school official in the nose, the hunch is that the definitions of accidents and/or incidents might well turn out to be somewhat adjusted by context.

Infuriated Teachers

Nothing infuriates teachers more than sending students to the office because of serious disciplinary or behavioral issues and the principal sending the students back to class within minutes. To make matters worse, some students return to class with a lollipop or licorice in hand.

Teachers have every right to expect their classrooms to be safe and that they will be supported in this expectation when students interrupt the learning environment. How much more should higher expectations of safety be appropriate with students who have histories of violence?

There are sometimes far too many accommodations made for students. Bureaucrats and politicians should pay close attention to the following:

> One of the more overused tools that frustrate teachers in all grades is the reliance on Individual Education Plans (IEPs). However, because we have established the culture of student-centrism, teachers must adjust all they do to the "learning needs" of each student. In terms of learning disorders and behavioral issues, "Students who have less-severe symptoms but who show limited academic progress because of BD (Bipolar Disorder) may benefit from a Section 504 plan, which might include specific accommodations and school-based counseling. An IEP is often created under the 'Emotional Disability' or 'Other Health Impaired' (OHI) category or disability, but for students to qualify for these services, their symptoms must adversely affect learning."[46]

EDUCATION AT A TIPPING POINT

Public education is at a serious tipping point. The extent of the problems in schools has reached new heights and now includes parents using social media in ways similar to those used by their children.[47] Most seem aware today of the nation's focus on the problems and solutions associated with bullying, but they are not aware of the physical assaults endured by teachers.

The overwhelming focus of bullying in schools is from student to student or group to student.[48] However, rapidly emerging are parents who engage in assaulting teachers and their reputations by means of the same social media platforms. These factors are enough for teachers to consider leaving the profession.

Teachers Leaving the Classrooms

These are serious moments for public education in America. Teachers are leaving the profession in large numbers. Some of these teachers are leaving due to economic reasons and the inability to find housing in their areas. In some geographic regions of the nation, particularly in inner cities where housing is in short supply, some schools are in such terrible condition that teachers fear for their safety.

In California alone, the *School Boards Association Survey* shows that teacher shortages exist in three-fourths of the state's school districts. Also, "of the approximately 238,000 people who quit teaching after the 2011–12 school year—the most recent data available—almost two-thirds left for reasons other than retirement."[49] This shortage directly affects teacher education programs negatively.

The numbers are pretty shocking. Teachers enrolled in teacher education programs around the nation "dropped from 691,000 to 451,000, a 35% reduction. . . . Fewer young people are interested in becoming teachers, and that's a problem because school enrollment is projected to increase by roughly three million students in the next decade."[50]

In areas where teachers are leaving the classrooms out of necessity, the nation must come to grips with issues faced by students and their parents. Some of the reasons teachers are leaving are because of threats to their safety as well as physical violence—and "they don't feel heard"[51] over many other issues.

Ironically, in some cities, teachers who have been restricted from the classrooms are finding their way back into the classrooms. Teachers unions and politicians are softening some of the restrictions of the past to work together to fill the classrooms with credentialed teachers who have a history of poor behaviors. As in the case of New York City, some criticize these actions as a new form of social justice on behalf of the needs of America's students and far too risky in placing bad teachers back in front of students. [52]

Policies and laws today in public education support the students over the teachers, especially if there is one or more specially protected categories with which districts have been specially charged with lessening discipline referrals. [53] The reality is that if teachers are not safe, then their students are not safe. If schools are unsafe, then imagine the fears of families as they send their children off into such environments.

Frightening Examples

Families are left to wonder in Minnesota after Como Park High School teacher Mark Rawlings was assaulted by two students. The district was slow in dealing with the assault. [54] Just a few months later, another teacher, John Ekblad, tried to break up a fight and was choked and body-slammed and lost consciousness. Ekblad still suffers from long-term residual physical ailments, such as numbness, vision problems, and headaches, according to his worker's compensation claim. [55]

A Few Questions Districts Must Answer

Education communities must establish clear policies regarding students who are verbally abusive or hit others, throw objects at classmates, or bully teachers. These policies must be written to address questions such as the following:

- Is a kindergartner's kicking of a teacher to be considered violence?
- How flagrant must an action be for the result to be considered an assault upon a teacher?
- Is there a school age that is considered too young to be considered an assailant?
- Does a teacher have to fear a lack of safety for her and her classroom?
- Is being injured just part of the job, especially when working with students with special needs or who are medicated or have violent home lives?
- Do actions have to be malicious and premeditated to constitute violence?
- How are schools and teachers to view impulses to be viewed as violent actions?
- In terms of determining whether students are truly violent, must there first be a track record of such actions?
- Are *patterns of violent behaviors* the only true actions of violence?
- If injuries occur, then is the definition of violence satisfied?

More and more teachers are on the receiving end of students' actions that cause injuries and result in unsafe school and hostile classroom environments for them and their students. When it comes to online practice, the new gossip is social media. Both Snapchat and Instagram, both of which allow posts and videos to disappear, bring attention to "hit-and-run" online assaults.

So far what has been presented advances the discussion and adds the notion of regular revisits of the definitions of violence and assault. When the Internet is added into the discussion, there is another consideration: *Does a person have to know he or she is harmed for an assault to be realized, or is it enough for others to understand that an assault has occurred, especially to one's character?*

VIOLENCE IN MANY FORMS

School violence extends to "several forms and can include bullying, intimidation, gang activity, locker theft, weapon use, assault—just about anything that results in a victim."[56] The same should be true when teachers step in to assist students and enhance campus safety. Teachers who are assaulted by students during student fights should be able to hold those students accountable for teacher injuries incurred.

In 2017, at Mecklinburg High School in North Carolina, fighting students "ended up injuring a teacher"[57] when the teacher tried to break up a fight and was assaulted. The district states that "some teachers get trained on how to break up fights, but it is advised to let Campus Security Associates or other security step in."[58] The principal at the school called the fight "an altercation" and disciplined the students according to the district's code of conduct for students. No arrests were made, even though during the previous 2016 school year, several personnel were also assaulted at the same school.[59]

At Cheltenham High School, which is a suburb of Philadelphia, students were charged and one was arrested after a fight broke out that resulted in serious injuries to teachers. One teacher was knocked unconscious. "Eight teachers at a high school in Pennsylvania were injured while breaking up a brawl between four female students. . . . One substitute teacher suffered a concussion."[60] In another case that garnered national attention, "Kevin Straub, a St. Louis, MO, teenager attacked his teacher so violently it triggered a stroke. The student was sentenced to 10 years in prison in 2014."[61]

Fights like those described above occur almost daily in some American public schools and often are recorded and posted to the Internet. Anecdotally, five fist fights broke out at the school at which this author is employed on the same day as this chapter was being edited. Social media was a major culprit in the assaults—one that involved a teacher and another that involved a security guard. The teacher in question has since attended the assailant's expulsion hearing.

Students video their classmates causing brawls in classes as well as their classmates sometimes punching teachers.[62] But these fights are by no means relegated to only schools in the United States. According to an independent research team in the United Kingdom, "some 20% of staff working in schools said they were attacked by pupils or parents during the 2010–2011 academic year."[63] Recording devices add fuel to the fire of those seeking online viral immortality.

The UK Is Not OK

The reality is that more and more teachers in a growing number of nations are now saying "they would not recommend a career in the classroom to family or friends."[64] Like the United States, the problem in the United Kingdom appears to be getting worse. In fact, a report by the Association of Teachers and Lecturers (ATL) has determined that nearly 50 percent "have been attacked or intimidated by pupils or parents."[65] The report continues:

> Teachers at all levels are experiencing "a rising tide of insults, threats and physical violence" amid warnings of a breakdown in respect towards adult authority. School personnel revealed a deterioration in standards of discipline from pupils and their parents in recent years, with claims that bad behavior was now becoming a "daily reality" for most staff and occupying far too much time. The UK study by the Association of Teachers and Lecturers found that more than half of teachers in state schools—57 percent—had been faced with aggression from a pupil in the last 12 months while a quarter had been confronted by angry mothers or fathers.
>
> Of those, more than eight-in-10 said the aggressive behavior from pupils took the form of insults, seven-in-10 said they had been intimidated or threatened and almost half had been physically attacked. The most common form of physical violence was pushing and shoving, but some teachers also reported pupils kicking, punching, spitting, scratching, biting, using furniture to launch assaults and even employing weapons such as knives.[66]

The most common forms of physical assaults against teachers in the UK included:

- Pushing or shoving
- Kicking
- Punching
- Spitting on
- Scratching
- Biting
- Throwing furniture

- Use of knives

Other actions that normally go unreported included:

- Students tossing liquids in the faces of teachers
- Parents refusing to accept the measures of discipline used toward their children
- Foul-mouthed parent profanities and berating the teacher, both in front of students
- Threats from parents to harm teachers
- Parents and students spreading gossip in the community and on social media, seeking to demean teachers

The United Kingdom is taking incremental steps toward regaining a semblance of authority. It is doing so by again empowering teachers. Contrast that with schools in the United States, where the bureaucrats and politicians—for fear of lawsuits—have continued to empower students and parents over teachers.

Teacher Assistants in the UK

The general trade union of the UK reported in June 2017 that there has been a rise in incidents of attacks being reported to the union. The union represents workers who would be considered blue collar, or classified workers at school, such as teachers' aides and classroom assistants.

In short, "54% of the teaching assistants say they have been physically abused or assaulted. Almost one in five—18% of the assistants polled, say they are attacked at least once a week. . . . Nearly a third—29% of the staff have been injured at school and more than one of five—21% say it has negatively affected their working life."[67]

Parallel this with cities in the United States, such as Oklahoma City, where "about 80 percent of district teachers who responded to a union survey said they are responsible for administering the majority of student discipline, while nearly half said they have a student with a chronic discipline problem who should not be in their classroom." The problems are not isolated.

It does seem, however, that the United Kingdom and the United States share a few things in common in terms of the concerns of teachers' assaults. Both agree that standards of behavior have "worsened in the last two years"[68] as well as "a deterioration over a longer, five-year period."[69] However, a divergence occurs when UK teachers are instructed to "use force to physically restrain unruly pupils, break-up fights and remove disruptive children from the classroom."[70]

The winds of education change with each new education director or political administration. Nothing could be closer to the truth than stating that policy differences exist between elected officials. The fact is that some American public schools are now places of police presence, metal detectors, and antigang units.

Some schools are tended to by racial and ethnic counselors and community liaisons. Some teachers are legally packing concealed weapons in some states. This author is not alone in the contention that these changes in education ought to send signals to communities that our schools are headed in very wrong directions.

Dozens and dozens of fight and assault videos have been posted by students, and many include teachers. Snapchat and Instagram postings and other social media platforms provide more than ample evidence that teachers are becoming injured more regularly by students. What should be done about these types of problems and others? If this is not the wrong direction for our schools, then there is probably no such thing.

ANOTHER SET OF PROGRAMS

Trauma-informed intervention and social-emotional learning are the newest education programs that target the whole child, which includes his or her behavior. They really are nothing new. Teachers and other professionals seek to understand why Generation Z children today act the way they do, especially the more challenging and emotionally disordered students. These programs seek to provide an understanding relevant to educating the whole child, including special needs students.

There are many intervention strategies that are on the market, and the majority of these strategies focus on shaping behaviors and mindsets. Some help by allowing students to reflect on themselves and think through their actions, both before and after these actions are taken.

Some aspects of these programs are reasonable and sensible. But are the expectations too high, and do they overpromise? Teachers who spend their time counseling and using creative tactics, with the intent to reduce official suspensions, spend less time teaching academics. The more time is taken in the classroom to deal with issues that distract from classroom learning, the less learning will occur.

Weak administrators, and even weaker laws protecting student perpetrators, are part of the larger problems associated with increases in violence against teachers. For example, students who are given time out of recess or sit in the office for a period before being released to the rest of their academic schedule are part of the wrong message sent to teachers. Student perpetrators, teachers, and their classes also receive the clear message.

Once the community discovers that students can injure teachers and remain in school with little threat of legal punishment, then the education system is further weakened. Is this where education in America is headed for the next few decades of the twenty-first century? If so, when this weakening is completely accomplished, students will understand their behaviors and actions can be expressed with near impunity.

Administrative Assistance

Protecting teachers does not begin once there is an injury. The spirit of protection is set long before by a school site administrator. It is incumbent upon each school site administrator to fashion policies and school culture that work for their campuses. Instituting zero tolerance for actions that harm teachers, whether substitutes or full-time staff employees, should be revisited.

The public must express that zero tolerance of violence at schools may help to regain control and stem the tide of violence against teachers as well as hold students accountable. Only then can school violence be reduced and result in safer schools for communities. This is the right direction for today's teachers.

WHAT NEEDS TO BE DONE

For teachers to perform their jobs effectively, they need to feel safe in their classrooms and with their students. There is no masking the fact that assaults against teachers are on the rise, leading to other serious problems in schools. Teachers are unable to defend themselves without fear of retribution from their administrators, their districts, and the parents. Teachers need to be able to defend themselves in classrooms.

School crimes are climbing each year, and the overall school environment is becoming more of a concern. Profanities are now commonplace. Words never heard before in public are now used with impunity. American culture is in need of a major overhaul, and families hold the key to this overhaul. Communities must support families, and families in turn must support schools.

Discipline policies must not favor students over teachers by providing multiple chances for similar offenses. They only reinforce poor behaviors for many students. Students today are quick to relate to adults that they cannot be touched or their parents will sue them. This arrogance emboldens students to act as they wish, all while being supported by legal protections and a litigious culture.

America is not the only nation to experience violence in epidemic proportions. However, we must learn from other nations' mistakes, and they must learn from ours. Families can help to change the culture of disobedience by holding their children accountable for actions outside the boundaries of appropriateness. Students come packaged with notions from home that impede the authority of the teacher, and this needs to change.

Teachers fear actions that would wrest authority from students and their desires. The immediacy of technological communication and parental complaints causes even teachers to minimize violence. In the face of being assaulted, parents and administrators will first ask what the teacher did to cause the student to lash out or injure someone. Teachers fear being blamed, so they take the assaults in stride. This needs to change, and district policies must be adopted that demonstrate support for teachers if they are assaulted.

Education is at a tipping point in the United States. Millions of students are no longer in the public school system. Parents do not want their children mixed in with all the issues that currently plague the American public education system. Social engineering, issues of safety, focus on identities, and politically based struggles over things not pertaining to academic achievement and preparation for careers have parents seeking alternative education models.

For this to change, communities have to begin rejecting some of the political decisions handed down that drive students away from public education. If not, teaching may become a contact sport, and classrooms will be full of potentially violent students, special needs students who have emotional and behavioral disorders, and the impoverished. Meanwhile, homeschools, private schools, and charter schools will continue to grow in interest.

States need to figure out what their core purpose of education is. If they cannot figure it out, then teachers will then question the best place to showcase their knowledge and skills for teaching.

NOTES

1. Samantha Hernandez. "Superintendent asks for community help with middle school." *USA Today.* June 28, 2017. Retrieved from www.greenbaypressgazette.com/story/news/education/2017/06/29/superintendent-asks-community-help-middle-school/436786001/.

2. Dorothy Espelage and Linda Reddy. "A silent national crisis: Violence against teachers." Brochure. *American Psychological Association.* 2016. Retrieved fromwww.apa.org/education/k12/teacher-victimization.aspx.

3. Institute of Education Sciences. *National Center for Education Statistics.* "School crime." 2013. Retrieved from https://nces.ed.gov/programs/digest/d15/tables/dt15_228.80.asp.

4. Dorothy Espelage, Eric M. Anderman, Veda Evanell Brown, et al. "Understanding and preventing violence directed against teachers." *American Psychological Association.* February–March 2013. Vol. 68, No. 2, 75–87 (viz. p. 76). Cf. also Dorothy Espelage and Linda Reddy. "A silent national crisis: Violence against teachers."

5. Simone Robers, Anlan Zhang, Rachel Morgan, et al. "Indicators of school crime and safety: 2014." (NCES 2015-072/NCJ 248036). *National Center for Education Statistics, US Department of Education, and Bureau of Justice Statistics, Office of Justice Programs, US*

Department of Justice. Washington, DC. 2015. Retrieved from http://nces.ed.gov and/or http://bjs.ojp.usdoj.gov.

6. Staff. "Report: School violence, bullying down in US public schools." *Associated Press*. July 27, 2017. Retrieved from https://apnews.com/73b134eca24142088c34da0531da4f63.

7. Jaclyn B. Kanrich. "Violence directed against educators: A critical review of findings and methodology." Doctoral Dissertation. Rutgers University, New Brunswick, New Jersey. October 2015. Retrieved from https://rucore.libraries.rutgers.edu/rutgers-lib/48191/.

8. Robers, Zhang, and Morgan, "Indicators of school crime and safety: 2014."

9. Randy Woods. "Trump economists say opioid crisis much bigger than envisioned." *Bloomberg Politics*. November 19, 2017. Retrieved from www.bloomberg.com/news/articles/2017-11-20/trump-economists-say-opioid-crisis-much-bigger-than-envisioned.

10. Staff. "What are the effects of secondhand exposure to marijuana smoke?" *National Institute on Drug Abuse*. August 2017. Retrieved from www.drugabuse.gov/publications/marijuana/what-are-effects-secondhand-exposure-to-marijuana-smoke.

11. Ibid.

12. Ibid.

13. Espelage, Anderman, and Brown, "Understanding and preventing violence directed against teachers."

14. Alex Ballinger. "7 out of 10 of Bristol teachers have been victims of violence at school." *The Bristol Post*. April 28, 2017. Retrieved from www.bristolpost.co.uk/news/bristol-news/7-out-10-bristol-teachers-37814.

15. Ibid.

16. Ibid.

17. Espelage, Anderman, and Brown, "Understanding and preventing violence directed against teachers."

18. Ibid.

19. Ibid.

20. Colette Hume. "Alarming number of teacher assaults, NUT Cymru says." *BBC Wales*. January 30, 2017. Retrieved from www.bbc.com/news/uk-wales-38761942.

21. Ibid.

22. Ibid.

23. Staff. "52% of SA teachers abused by pupils." *EyeWitness News*. March 2013. Retrieved from http://ewn.co.za/2013/10/02/521-teachers-exposed-to-verbal-abuse. Cf. Patrick Burton and Lezanne Leoschut. "School violence in South Africa: Results of the 2012 national school violence study." *Centre for Justice and Crime Prevention*. March 2013. Retrieved from www.cjcp.org.za/uploads/2/7/8/4/27845461/monograph12-school-violence-in-south_africa.pdf.

24. David O'Leary. "£290k paid out to Scots teachers for assaults and injuries." *The Scotsman*. January 6, 2016. Retrieved from www.scotsman.com/news/education/290k-paid-out-to-scots-teachers-for-assaults-and-injuries-1-3992711.

25. Ibid.

26. Editors. "Teach me if you can: Why violence against teachers in Germany is on the rise." *Sputnik News Europe*. November 21, 2016. Retrieved from https://sputniknews.com/europe/201611211047670495-violence-teachers-germany/.

27. Ibid.

28. Adam Boult. "Shocking footage shows teacher in brutal fight with students." *The Telegraph*. April 22, 2016. Retrieved fromwww.telegraph.co.uk/news/2016/04/22/shocking-footage-shows-teacher-in-brutal-fight-with-students/.

29. Ibid.

30. Ibid.

31. Ibid.

32. Sara Malm. "Classroom horror as Chinese pupil kills teacher for confiscating his mobile by slitting his throat." *Daily Mail*. September 17, 2013. Retrieved fromwww.dailymail.co.uk/news/article-2423913/Chinese-pupil-kills-teacher-classroom-confiscating-mobile-phone.html.

33. Ibid.

34. Bethany Hiatt. "15yo student facing assault charges after allegedly punching a teacher." *The West Australian.* October 25, 2016. Retrieved from https://thewest.com.au/news/wa/15yo-student-facing-assault-charges-after-allegedly-punching-a-teacher-ng-ya-121653.

35. Ibid.

36. Ibid.

37. Callie Watson. "Five teachers a day assaulted by students." *Adelaide Now.* July 16, 2012. Retrieved from www.adelaidenow.com.au/news/south-australia/five-teachers-a-day-assaulted-by-students/news-story/552486cc375fc936f1bf2e27fa4933fd?sv=c4f72d0a1f695623cac67ed88ccc18aa.

38. Gosia Sawicka. "Dozens of school staff, teachers assaulted in Winnipeg in past two years." *CBC News.* January 15, 2015. Retrieved from www.cbc.ca/news/canada/manitoba/iteam/dozens-of-school-staff-teachers-assaulted-in-winnipeg-in-past-2-years-1.2901178.

39. Ibid.

40. Ibid.

41. Linda A Reddy, Dorothy L. Espelage, Susan D. McMahon, et al. "Violence against teachers: Case studies from the APA Task Force." December 4, 2013. *International Journal of School & Educational Psychology*, Vol. 1, Number 4, pp. 231–245 (viz. p. 243). Retrieved from http://www.tandfonline.com/doi/full/10.1080/21683603.2013.837019. Cf. Dorothy L. Espelage, Mrinalini A. Rao, and Rhonda G. Craven in Sherrie Bauman, Donna Cross, and Jenny Walker (Eds.). 2013. "Theories of Cyberbullying (Chapter 5)." *Principles of cyberbullying research: Definitions, measures, and methodology.* New York, NY: Routledge Press, pp. 49–67. Cf. Also, Ernest J. Zarra, III. *Teacher-student relationships: Crossing into the emotional, physical, and sexual realms.* 2013. See pp. 99–123.

42. Ibid., all.

43. Peter Tait. "Causes of growing mental health problems sit largely within schools." *The Telegraph.* December 2, 2015. Retrieved from www.telegraph.co.uk/education/educationopinion/12025711/Schools-largely-to-blame-for-rising-mental-health-issues.html. Cf. Nancy Colier. "What to do about the people who blame you for everything." *Psychology Today.* December 13, 2015. Retrieved from www.psychologytoday.com/blog/inviting-monkey-tea/201512/what-do-about-the-people-who-blame-you-everything.

44. Derek Hawkins. "Oregon man carries mother's severed head into a grocery store, stabs a clerk." May 16, 2017. *The Washington Post.* Retrieved from https://www.washingtonpost.com/news/morning-mix/wp/2017/05/16/oregon-man-carries-mothers-severed-head-into-a-grocery-then-stabs-a-clerk-police-say/?utm_term=.583e07c69aea. Cf. George Houde. "Man who beheaded mom in 2003 gets transfer from Elgin mental hospital." *Chicago Tribune.* October 13, 2017. Retrieved from http://www.chicagotribune.com/suburbs/elgin-courier-news/news/ct-man-killed-mother-seeks-elgin-release-met-20160204-story.html.

45. Staff. "Symptoms and accommodations." *Juvenile Bipolar Research Foundation.* No date. Retrieved from www.jbrf.org/page-for-families/educational-issues-facing-children-with-bipolar-disorder/symptoms-and-accomodations/.

46. J. Elizabeth Chesno Grier, Megan L. Wilkins, and Carolyn Ann Stirling Pender. "Bipolar disorder: Educational implications for secondary students." *National Association of School Psychologists*, p. 13. April 2007. Retrieved from www.nasponline.org/Documents/Resources%20and%20Publications/Handouts/Families%20and%20Educators/bipolar.pdf.

47. Taylor Hatmaker. "A huge survey shows that teens are bullied most on Instagram and Facebook." *Tech Crunch.* July 20, 2017. Retrieved from https://techcrunch.com/2017/07/19/ditch-the-label-2017-cyberbullying-report/.

48. Robert Preidt. "Bullying takes financial toll on U.S. school districts." *Health Day.* July 6, 2017. Retrieved from https://consumer.healthday.com/kids-health-information-23/bullying-health-news-718/bullying-takes-financial-toll-on-u-s-school-districts-724168.html.

49. Stephen Wall. "Is housing built for teachers a solution to California's staffing shortage?" *Press Enterprise.* July 2, 2017. Retrieved from www.pe.com/2017/07/02/bill-would-help-pay-for-teacher-housing/.

50. Patrick J. Kearney. "Where are all of the teachers going?" *Huffington Post.* July 16, 2017. Retrieved from www.huffingtonpost.com/entry/where-are-all-the-teachers-going_us_596b7e10e4b06a2c8edb474c.

51. Ibid.

52. Staff. "City hall's rush to put bad teachers back in the classroom." *New York Post.* July 10, 2017. Retrieved from http://nypost.com/2017/07/10/city-halls-rush-to-put-bad-teachers-back-in-the-classroom/.

53. Juanita Chavez. "Historic settlement reached in lawsuit against Kern High School District, 7/26/17." *Dolores Huerta Foundation.* August 11, 2017. Retrieved from http://doloreshuerta.org/historic-settlement-reached-in-lawsuit-against-kern-high-school-district-72617/.

54. Editorial Board. "If teachers aren't safe, students aren't safe." *Star Tribune.* March 11, 2016. Retrieved from www.startribune.com/if-teachers-aren-t-safe-students-aren-t-safe/371846501/.

55. Josh Verges. St. Paul teacher's lawsuit over Central high assault dismissed." *Twin Cities Pioneer Press.* May 25, 2017. Retrieved from www.twincities.com/2017/05/25/ekblad-judge-dismisses-st-paul-teachers-lawsuit-over-central-high-assault/.

56. Dorothy Espelage, Eric M. Anderman, Veda Evanell Brown, et al. "Understanding and preventing violence directed against teachers." February–March 2013. *American Psychologist.* Vol. 68, No. 2, pp. 75–87 (viz. p. 76).

57. Dedrick Russell. "Teacher assaulted while breaking up fight involving students." *WBTV Charlotte.* April 28, 2017. Retrieved from www.wbtv.com/story/35279312/video-teacher-assaulted-while-breaking-up-fight-involving-students.

58. Ibid.

59. Ibid.

60. Stephanie Haney. "Eight teachers are injured after trying to break up wild girl fight caught on video in school hallway." *Daily Mail.* May 4, 2017. Retrieved from www.dailymail.co.uk/news/article-4474772/Eight-teachers-injured-trying-break-wild-girl-fight.html.

61. Editorial Board. "If teachers aren't safe, students aren't safe." *Star Tribune.* March 11, 2016. Retrieved from www.startribune.com/if-teachers-aren-t-safe-students-aren-t-safe/371846501/.

62. Rebecca Klopf. "Video shows Milwaukee teen punching teacher." *ABC News.* August 22, 2017. Retrieved from www.tmj4.com/news/national/milwaukee-teen-arrested-for-punching-teacher-1.

63. Graeme Paton. "One-in-five teachers have been 'physically attacked' at school." *The Telegraph.* September 2, 2011. Retrieved from www.telegraph.co.uk/education/educationnews/8735837/One-in-five-teachers-physically-attacked-at-school.html.

64. Ibid.

65. Graeme Paton. "Threats and assaults becoming a 'daily reality' for teachers." *The Telegraph.* September 1, 2014. Retrieved from www.telegraph.co.uk/education/educationnews/11068449/Threats-and-assaults-becoming-a-daily-reality-for-teachers.html.

66. Ibid.

67. Jamie Doward. "Most school support staff have been assaulted by pupils." *The Guardian.* June 2, 2017. Retrieved from www.theguardian.com/education/2017/jun/03/most-school-support-staff-assaulted-by-pupils-union-survey.

68. Paton, "Threats and assaults becoming a 'daily reality' for teachers."

69. Ibid.

70. Paton, "One-in-five teachers have been 'physically attacked' at school."

Chapter Three

Has Teaching Become a Contact Sport?

Many pre-service teachers aren't necessarily equipped with the skills to manage their classrooms. So, it starts with preservice education. This is a priority in special education, where teachers are really taught how to deescalate conflict. . . . Teachers cannot perform their job effectively if they feel threatened. [1]

Teachers are frustrated because they continue to have to toggle between what is best for student learning and the federal and state education mandates. These frustrations are addressed in a previous book, *Common Sense Education: From Common Core to ESSA and Beyond.* American teachers are trying to come to terms with a bureaucracy that is stripping educators' rights of protection and replacing them with decisions that result in protections moving away from teachers. This is not sensible.

Educational ideologies are never enough to compensate for the practical realities faced by teachers in their classrooms. Officials must be made to understand this, and they need to adopt sensible policies going forward. What officials also must contend with is a culture that has become flagrantly more physical.

PUNCHED OUT OR BURNED OUT?

When six Carson, Nevada, middle school girls invited other public school students, through an online posting, to take part in "Attack a Teacher Day," they were arrested. Eighteen students had signed on for the attack. Soon after, a parent alerted authorities about the students who signaled their intention to join in the mass assault on teachers at their schools.

On the same day the six girls were arrested, "17-year old student Robert Butler walked into Millard South High School in Omaha, Nebraska, and shot his principal and assistant principal. Butler later committed suicide, and the assistant principal, Vicki Kaspar, died of her wounds."[2]

Additional stories abound involving assaults of teachers, damage to property, and even deaths.[3] Here are a few examples:

- A twelve-year-old student from Surprise, Arizona, smashed teachers with a computer keyboard and kicked and punched them until restrained by a police officer.
- In Manchester, New Hampshire, an eighth-grade student body-slammed a teacher and injured her so badly that she was left immobile, without crutches.
- A substitute teacher in Pittsburgh, Pennsylvania, lost hearing in one ear and suffered head trauma and blurred vision after one of a group of students tossed an M-80 explosive into a vacant classroom where the substitute teacher was reading.
- In St. Louis, Missouri, a fourth-grade teacher collapsed and died of a heart attack after a physical assault and prolonged altercation with a nine-year-old.

In another example, in St. Paul, Minnesota, a "55-year-old Central High School teacher was choked into unconsciousness after trying to break up a fight that started over an argument about football statistics. When the teacher intervened, a 16-year-old student allegedly picked up the teacher and slammed him into a table and chair, before slamming him to the floor. The teacher passed out for 10 to 20 seconds."[4]

In April 2016, the St. Paul school went on the offensive and claimed the injured teacher was at fault by trying to break up a fight, when a third party, not under the control of the students fighting in the school's cafeteria, hit the teacher and caused his injuries. The district argued that the teacher, John Ekblad, was "careless and negligent, but that his injuries were caused by third persons over whom the defendants had no control."[5]

Eventually, the lawsuit against the district was thrown out for several reasons, not the least of which is the fact that cases like Ekblad's are already handled through worker's compensation. The teenage student in question, which Ekblad claimed caused the career-ending injuries, "pleaded guilty to third-degree felony assault and was given 90 days of home monitoring and community service. He told a judge he was trying to stop a fight involving his younger brother when Ekblad grabbed him from behind."[6] Are we at the point where teachers should just allow students to knock each other around and wait until security arrives? At this point, the moral and legal considerations are at odds with each other. Even the law, which is supposed to protect students, is failing them.

SAME OLD FRESH START?

Heading into any new school year is exciting, and teachers look forward to fresh starts. However, far too many teachers bear the wounds of previous years of abuse. Certainly, many teachers are resilient and have an uncanny and innate ability to step back and view things from a distance. Still, the fact remains, we have an untold number of recovering assault victims teaching in our schools.

Teachers are excellent at compartmentalizing experiences and emotions. However, burying the past for a new year or two may rear its ugly head at certain points in the near future. The act of being punched out may well lead to burn out and migration of good teachers away from the profession they love.

When teachers complain about being burned out, this phenomenon may well find its genesis in the mindset of starting afresh in the fall. Carrying the emotional burden from previous years of unresolved issues builds up. How many teachers bury their yesterdays in the busyness of their todays? From all indications, the data are clear that teachers underreport the events they experience in the classroom. [7]

Teacher burnout is not just an outcome. Burnout is the result of an accumulation of stress and its effects, pressing more and more teachers to their tipping points. This includes newer teachers as well as veteran teachers. The increased fear of violence by teachers certainly adds to this accumulation of stress for new and veteran teachers alike.

HAS TEACHING BECOME A CONTACT SPORT?

Has teaching become a new *contact sport*? Students and parents physically injure hundreds to thousands of teachers annually. Teachers who also coach have another level of abuse they sometimes experience. Crowds at games are full of boisterous and often obnoxious fans. This brings its own set of ramifications.

Along with veteran teachers, even substitute teachers are being assaulted by students. For example, in Antioch, California, "a 13-year-old girl at Antioch Middle School punched a substitute teacher multiple times in the face and continued hitting the woman after she was on the ground." [8] What could incite a student to act without fear of consequences for assaulting a teacher?

In terms of the degree of concern applied to student violence in general, there is evidence that the problem is widespread. However, states view the matter differently and handle it differently. For example, the question is left up to New Jersey administrators as to whether there is a "suspension or expulsion," [9] depending on the severity of the incident.

The state Education Code "identifies a handful of offenses that call for a principal to recommend expulsion, but it also allows him to make exceptions."[10] The public often yields to their emotions and calls for expulsion of a violent-acting student or one who is a danger to others. "Administrators tend to have a different perspective."[11] In a recent New Jersey case, what made it unique was that a teacher fought back against his attackers.

From the parking lots, where teachers' cars and personal property are damaged by disgruntled students and parents, to the punches, kicks, slaps, and thrown objects in classes—to students being sent right back to our classrooms after major incidents—teachers have endured abuse. This has to end. Teachers must continue to share their stories and band together in providing professional and personal support to help end this scourge of assaults in culture.

PARENTS VERSUS TEACHERS

Taking sides has become a favorite pastime for Americans, especially with politics and sports. There is no exception to this when it comes to education. With violence in schools, as long as parents model aggressive defiance for their children, they can expect their children to demonstrate the same. Along with other external forces in culture, if this negative modeling doesn't change, the problems in schools will worsen. The following excerpt illustrates the point:

> Aggressive and highly competitive parents usually are heavily involved in their children's lives. They practice regular communication with schools, sometimes over minuscule issues. They are heavy-handed in the selection of their children's teachers, classes, clubs, and sports. This type of parenting crosses all generations and has been a hallmark of the control-type parent for as long as anyone can remember. *There are differences between helicopter and bulldozer parents.* . . . Some helicopter parents have decided to land, and this group has begun to earn another moniker. The goal for this newer group is to score points on behalf of their children. . . . When bulldozer parents finish driving home their points, there is little left standing between people. Not only are these parents able to get their way, but they plow over anyone who stands in their way. Bulldozer parents are a win-at-all-cost group.[12]

As an example of struggling with the typical Gen Z bulldozer parent today, a Baby Boomer shares:

> I was a witness to this in my home state, just a few years back. The bulldozer parent overlaps into personal interactions as well. God forbid that your child got into some altercation or disagreement with the child of a bulldozer parent. In my particular subsection of the county, I was the rare single parent in a

group of many bulldozer two-parent households. Having said that, I eventually had to become a bulldozer parent when dealing with public school administration and fighting to get the proper services for my older son after spending almost $100,000 on private education for three years when, in sixth grade, the school tested him and said he did not need services. After spending an additional $6,000 on private testing and multiple thousands on an educational advocate, and getting pissed off that I had to go to such great lengths to get my son what he needed, I came back fighting and had to turn into a bulldozer parent. But that was only with respect to advocating for my disabled son's proper education. [13]

TRENDING VIOLENCE NEEDS A RESPONSE

In 2016, at Wooddale High School, Memphis, Tennessee, a sixteen-year-old art student was instructed not to leave the classroom and go out into the hallway. After being egged on by some of his classmates, each with cell phones at the ready, the sixteen-year-old student walked up behind the teacher, Mark Kennell.

The student hit the teacher, wrestled with him, and eventually knocked him to the ground. Apparently, several troublemaking students were making it a practice to attack teachers and even jump parents so they could record the assaults and post them online. The assault in question was planned in advance by the student. [14] These kinds of assaults are beginning to come across as some sort of competitive game.

Since 2006, there have been assault reports, and arrests have climbed steadily in Chicago's public schools. It was during that year that Norma Brown, an elementary school teacher, asked a fourth-grade student to remove his hat in the lunchroom. "A fight ensued. A group of 11- and 12-year-olds surrounded Brown, yelling and cursing. One cocked his fist and hit her squarely in the left eye.

"Brown stumbled for the door. Simultaneously, two girls, a sixth-grader and an eighth-grader, began punching and kicking her. She fought to regain standing. 'I knew that if I fell to the ground they would stomp me. . . . When you fall, you're dead meat.'" [15]

Like many other inner cities in America, there are trends of violence in schools. Chicago, Illinois, is no exception. As a result of the attack on Brown, a thirty-year veteran teacher at the time, she had to leave teaching and suffers from post-traumatic stress disorder (PTSD). Her career in the classroom has ended.

As far as her colleagues and others are concerned, they fear for their safety as well. "Violent crimes are a daily occurrence in many troubled Chicago Public Schools. Police log dozens of calls a week from CPS schools, investigating complaints of battery, drug use, armed robberies, sexual assault, bomb threats and arson. In this environment . . . it is possible that even teachers who have never been attacked can suffer symptoms of PTSD. They may feel anxious or on edge."[16]

In Burleson, Texas, seventeen-year-old Dylan Brown refused to go to class. When approached by a teacher and asked why he was not in class, Brown shoved the teacher. The teacher fell back and hit a doorknob. The injury was not serious, but an assault occurred. The student was charged with felony assault.[17]

Confronting some students and doing one's job as a teacher can result in physical injury. In another example, a mother of a special education student at the John Muir Middle School in South Los Angeles became angry that her seventh-grade child was not allowed to wear her hoodie in class. The teacher explained that wearing the hoodies in class violated school policy. The special education teacher was beat up for several minutes by the parent and her daughter. The teacher, who remains anonymous, stated, "I was not trained for this, this is not what I signed up for."[18]

THE FEAR OF BEING BLAMED

Administrators are often on a career path and look forward to seeking positions of greater responsibility. If they began as classroom teachers, there is an understanding of what teachers face. However, with many years between administrators' classroom experiences and their daily regimen associated with their daily administrative responsibilities, there exists a serious disconnect.

Often, while saying they support teachers, this disconnect results in taking sides with policymakers and bureaucrats as well as parents and fellow administrators. For many, this sequence of disconnect is a natural next sequence in moving up the ladder of authority. At some point, administrators no longer practice complete support of teachers only. This diminished support usually results in compromise of teacher authority.

School site administrators who make waves might embarrass the school board and the districts involved. Many states give these administrators discretion and options to keep students in school rather than move toward zero tolerance of repeat and chronic offenders.

That is all well and good for the administrator, who has probably not been in the classroom teaching for several years and has not observed the changes that have taken place with smart technology. Social media and student behaviors and disruptions are now more wedded to the preadolescent and teenage years.

An example of an administrator losing sight of the plights of teachers is found in Florida. A teacher is blamed for escalating a situation, resulting in her own assault. An administrator who sides with a parent in one meeting and the teacher in another is a spineless administrator. For the record, the taking of sides against the middle is an example of how administrators succumb to the natural course of shifting alliances—and the quickest way to lose respect among teachers.

Blaming a teacher for her own assault is unconscionable. Should other serious crimes against teachers come with the same blame? "A Pinellas County School teacher was roughed-up by a student, and instead of the principal taking up for the teacher—she blamed her."[19] The school surveillance video showed the assaulted teacher blocking the classroom door after she had sent a student to the office for classroom disruptions.

The principal, Wendy Bryan, "saw the video and blamed the teacher for starting it and should have let the student into the classroom instead of blocking his way."[20] An aide who came to assist the teacher was also knocked to the ground and had his keys stolen by the assailant. Bryan said, "the aide should have handed over his keys."[21] However, the school resource officer stated that the teacher used the self-defense tactics and techniques for which she was trained by the district.[22]

Here is another example, this time from a private school teacher claiming to have been verbally abused by her principal and blamed for an incident she endured.

> Hi teacher friends! I need some prayer (and willing to take some advice too!) My principal was gossiping about me to one of my coworkers. I asked him if there's a problem to please come to me instead of my coworkers. He then proceeded to scream at me for 10 minutes while I sat and sobbed uncontrollably in his office. He told me that he was justified to talk about me because I was rude to him (not sure when . . .). He also told me that I was replaceable. . . . My heart is broken into a million pieces. I've worked with my principal for 3 years and never had any problems so I'm so confused and hurt by what happened. . . . My heart is so torn. I feel like leaving is not best for my students but I also feel like there's no recovering from your principal screaming at you. Prayers and advice welcome please![23]

Often, the unfortunate part of working at some private schools is that there is no outside group that has your back. When situations arise, as they do in both private and public education, private school employees can be sent packing without recourse. At-will contracts are also the hallmark of most charter schools as well. Assaults come at teachers from all angles and from all corners, and it makes little difference whether schools are public or private.

WHO SHARES THE BLAME?

Over the years, the blame for out-of-control students has been placed on parents, schools, teachers, drugs, technology, friends, and even the change in the climate. Society has been slow to blame the children themselves for the actions that result in today's explosions of assaults at schools of teachers and fellow students.

Reading through comment after comment on articles posted on teachers' blogs and school websites, it is apparent that teachers and parents are saddled with much blame for the way students are today. For example, in Lehigh Valley, Pennsylvania, there was a report that multiple teachers had "been assaulted over the last few months,"[24] beginning in February 2017.

The community sounded off with the following comments, many of which appeared on a community comment page. The comments include those from teachers, administrators, parents, and community members. A sample of these comments is listed below. Take note of the areas of blame.

- "This is why the schools no longer teach but put their noses in people's homes . . . because of nit wit parents not disciplining their kids. . . . Expel them and make the parents pay for their little darling's private school."
- "In all fairness they are sticking children with autism and emotional disorders in large classes (with) not enough teachers. This is hard for the children . . . and the ones with the disorders."
- "We as teachers are there to educate, not parent the students—that is up to the parents at home to take care of their children and their emotional needs. But if the family is truly dysfunctional that's exactly what we are going to receive in school—dysfunctional students."
- "This . . . could have been written about schools all over the country. I wish I knew how to remedy these situations. I'm reminded that we have to deal with the students we have, not the ones we used to have."
- "It's not always the parent's fault . . . a child can actually just be disturbed, so fining and punishing a parent is ridiculous. Kids need to be punished. It is the teacher's job when the kids are at school . . . expel kids."
- "This occurs because the hands of the teachers are tied when it comes to discipline. Parents are suing the district and even worse, not parenting at home. If the students think this type of behavior is acceptable in school it is most likely because it is acceptable at home."
- "This is a huge problem. Obviously, the parents need to do more to get on their kids. But first, the school system needs to stop allowing it. The more you tolerate, the more the problem grows."
- "A lot of these kids are in emotional support classes with different diagnoses. It's just not your average misbehaving kids. A lot of them have IEPs and are in special therapy and other special programs as well."
- "Maybe it's time we stop slapping kids on the hand and send them to the police to show them what they get when they aren't protected by their school laws."

- "Kids' bad behavior starts at home when parents abuse kids, whether it is physically or verbally. Continued punishment and being grounded a lot takes a toll on a child's mind."
- "Everyone is blaming the parents. These kids sound like they may have some sort of problem with anxiety—or even worse, severe like autism."
- "Hold the parents responsible. Mandatory 3-day lock up, during the work week so they miss work."
- "What happened to expelling, or at least suspending the unruly student? This situation is so unfair to the teachers who want to teach, the students who want to learn, and the taxpayers whose money is being wasted."
- "I guess you need to take a look at their parents and role models, young poorly educated thug types!"
- "Don't worry. They're smart. And will walk out on a VP commencement speech some day and be considered wonderful."

EMPOWERMENT OF GROUPS

Empowering one or more groups over others to pad statistics or to score political points is not educational success. Students will flaunt every loophole possible and then expect that consequences will favor them when they are involved in altercations. Hans Bader seemed to predict our current status.

> The Obama Administration signaled that it will hold school districts liable for such racial disparities under federal Title VI regulations. In the long run, the only practical way for school districts to comply with this guidance is to tacitly adopt unconstitutional racial quotas in school discipline. This will result in increased school violence, discrimination in discipline against White and Asian students, and increased racial achievement gap that harms Black students, and more public colleges will be affected, not just school districts, since Title VI bans racial discrimination not just in the public schools, but in higher education as well. The administration made it clear that it views racial disparities in student discipline rates, which exist in virtually all school systems, as generally being the product of racism by school officials. . . . The Supreme Court ruled in *United States v. Armstrong* (1996) that there is no "legal presumption" that all races commit all types of crimes at the same rate, since that is "contradicted by" real world data.[25]

Bader, who was left in a brain-injured condition after an assault by a student, "has accused the Obama administration of creating racial quotas in school discipline."[26] He and others are poised to see a rollback of the Obama-era limitations on school discipline policy. The Trump administration has moved forward, and "researchers and policy experts on both sides of the debate are bracing for a big reversal that will deal a major blow to civil rights groups."[27]

Bader also addresses the effects of the Obama-era racial recalibration policies. Recently, Evergreen College, in Washington State, had a "White people free day"[28] on campus. This caused some to accuse the group holding the event as "fascist mercenaries who physically intimidate and sometimes actually do violence to those whose ideas they do not like."[29]

One professor, Bret Weinstein, was targeted because of his objection to the day and was told not to show up back on campus that day due to safety reasons. The student organizers of the event claim that "We deemed that the video created for the Day of Absence and Day of Presence . . . was stolen by White supremacists and edited to expose and ridicule the students and staff."[30]

Walter Williams, a Black professor of economics at George Mason University shares his perspective:

> School violence is going to get worse. . . . [T]he Obama Administration sent all the school districts in the country a letter warning them to avoid racial bias when suspending or expelling students. Secretary of Education Arne Duncan claimed that racial discrimination in the administration of discipline is a real problem today. . . . In Washington, D.C., an official of a teacher's union tried to explain to a national gathering of black elected officials why white teachers are so problematic for black students, saying they just do not understand black culture. Excuses and calls for leniency will embolden school thugs. . . . The sorry and tragic state of black education and its attendant problems will not be turned around until there's a change in what's acceptable behavior and what's unacceptable behavior. That change must come from the black community.[31]

CURRENT PERCEPTIONS

Currently, a growing number of the American public view race relations negatively. Whether it is the National Football League, urban communities, or public schools, factional dissent based on race is reminiscent of the mid-1960s.

The summer prior to the election of 2016, seven in ten Americans viewed "race relations in the United States as poor—nearly matching a record high. In the wake of a white nationalist demonstration in Charlottesville, Virginia . . . 28 percent of the public—including 24 percent of whites and 40 percent of African-Americans—say that race relations are 'very bad,' with another 42 percent of all respondents calling them 'fairly' bad."[32]

Some voters viewed the election of Donald Trump as president as a racial backlash to having the first president of color. Some saw it as a possibility to counteract Barack Obama's policies.[33] Others saw nothing but blatant racism the reason for his election and subsequent statements about various groups of people.[34] Whatever the conclusion, this has spilled over into culture and has not produced better relations among races.

Cultural Changes

Whether in curriculum, state standards, or the media's portrayals of the world, teachers tend to perceive changes in culture first. Culture enters their classrooms, and they help to shape it and sort it. Teachers understand that what culture shapers create soon marches into America's classrooms at all levels.[35] The age of the smartphone brings with it ubiquity on several levels; some of this is positive and some is negative. Many teachers continue to search for the positive.

Another example of growing intolerance leading to violence comes by way of higher education. Allison Stanger, a political science professor at Middlebury College, in Vermont, was assigned to escort a controversial special speaker across campus. Violent student protesters forbid the speech and assaulted Professor Stanger by pulling her hair and injuring her neck as she escorted the speaker, Charles Murray, to his car. The agitators pounded on his car as he sought to drive away.

Bullying and violent incidents such as these are on the rise across America. Every day, it seems, headlines present another case of a protected class lashing out. From safe spaces to inner-city crime zones, it is as if protected-class groups sense they have been empowered to run roughshod across those with whom they refuse to allow the First Amendment to apply equally.[36] There is one significant point that is required here. The First Amendment does not protect violent expressions.

ABOVE REPROACH?

Communities need to be certain that teachers are not part of the continuing causes of the violence directed at them. As a result, those who stand before our nation's students should be of high importance, and their safety should be paramount. Conversely, to whom much is given, much is required. Accountability for teachers is of equal importance. (See chapter 6 for additional discussion.)

Parents and students deserve well-trained professionals to educate in our schools. How can Americans tell whether teachers are well qualified? To begin, *USA Today* has assembled all of the states' credential websites for the public to verify the credentials and certifications of teachers. Everyone is encouraged to navigate the website to view the names of teachers in schools and their credentials. Your state can be found at the following link: www. usatoday.com/story/news/2016/02/13/state-teacher-background-lookup-resources/80355350/.[37]

EDUCATIONAL EQUITY

All across the United States, schools are succumbing to lawsuits in the name of educational equity. This means students who would never have been placed in a regular education classroom just a few years ago are now being included in greater numbers in regular education programs. Inclusion is a new education buzzword. Education, as a whole, must take care not to be so politically correct that it perpetuates educational incompetence. Some education policies that come down from bureaucrats are real head-scratchers.

Jane Meredith Adams characterizes this: "As California presses school districts to stop suspending hundreds of thousands of students a year, many teachers . . . say they have been under-prepared for the change, according to a new survey by the California Teachers Association. . . . Nearly 8 out of 10 teachers surveyed said they need more training and the support of school psychologists and counselors if they are to successfully retreat from 'zero tolerance' discipline practices, in which even minor infractions may result in a student being sent home for a day or more."[38]

Restorative Justice Programs

President of the California Teachers Association (CTA), Eric Heins, believes that "Restorative and positive practices are the right direction to go . . . referring to restorative practices that allow students to make amends and to programs that teach positive social and emotional skills to provide counseling and interventions."[39] At first glance, this appears sensible. What is being discovered is vastly different.

According to Heins, what is being discovered is that "students are being thrown back into the classroom and nothing has been done to deal with their behavior. . . . Eighty-six percent of the nearly 3,500 teachers and other staff who completed an online survey between May and December 2016 said they need additional training in how to reach the students they once sent to the office, as well as increased access to mental health professionals to support students in distress."[40]

Some of the comments by California teachers, which were posted in the Meredith article, indicate that not all CTA members who are currently teaching agree with the direction the state board of education is headed. Likewise, the same sentiments are applicable to some in leadership at the CTA. Observe the following sample comments:[41]

- "I am thankful this is my very last year of teaching in California. The infinite wisdom of Sacramento strikes again. I as a teacher am supposed to allow some malcontent to disrupt the learning environment and sabotage everyone else's education. What would the politicians do to a disrupter who tried to sabotage their legislative process? Why, have them removed of course. More double standards as usual." (Dave)

- "Developmental trauma changes the architecture of the physical brain, ability to learn and social behavior. It impacts 2 out of 3 children at some level, but I didn't even know what it was." (Daun)
- "Seems that most any problem, whether educational, psychological, socio-economic, or medical, can apparently be solved by having trained teachers receive more training and sit through more seminars." (Raoul)
- "For a school to work, a student must adhere to a modicum of basic behavior guidelines without which the class cannot proceed with learning." (Don)

Who Bears the Burden?

One of the problems with placing the brunt of suspensions and expulsion reductions on teachers is placing them on the frontline of accountability. Who or what is helping parents to hold their own kids accountable for their actions? Why is it the school's responsibility to correct behaviors that originate at home? Why should teachers act as the parents to their students?

Teachers are not trained in psychotherapy. Most took a limited number of psychology classes in undergraduate and credential programs. Teachers are nominal behavior modifiers for large groups and not behavior controllers. Students must learn to self-regulate and control their own behaviors.

This self-regulation remains difficult when there are few affective filters, weakened discipline policies, and multiple poor behavior trigger points that exist in classrooms. Students do not necessarily need incentives to misbehave. But given incentives to do so, one had better stand back and take cover.

Parents must teach control to their children, first and foremost. If students are unable to control their behaviors, then they should be removed from the environment until they can control themselves. Their lack of self-control must not be allowed to encourage others to resort to the same behaviors. After all, actions without consequences teach the wrong message, both at home and at school.[42]

WHAT NEEDS TO BE DONE

At a time when it seems American culture is swamped with allegations of assault, one would think that there would be encouragement from politicians, bureaucrats, and administrators for teachers to report assaults against them. The truth is that in many schools in the United States, there are teachers and students whose lives are being affected by school violence. Sometimes, the effects of this violence are an extension of the home lives of the students.

The nation's most precious resource, its children, are growing up in a culture that is desensitized to violence because it seems to surround them at every turn. Students contact it on the Internet. They contact it on television, and they experience others contacting it as well. Teachers come in contact with it in the classroom and on the Internet. Unfortunately, this contact is becoming more physical and injurious, all while recorded by students in efforts to compete with others for viral video status.

Several things need to occur for our students to understand that violence against anyone is unacceptable, and this includes their teachers. First, parents must be educated as to the dangers of repeating violence in front of their children. Local and state politicians must go to parent–school meetings and address the issues.

Second, students need to be advised that unacceptable behaviors will be dealt with swiftly. Restricting students from school, from athletic participation, and from any school events must be implemented. This includes for verbal assaults and physical assaults. Students must be taught that fighting and injuring others is the lowest form of dealing with problems and it should be made illegal. This should go hand in hand with countering bullying at school, and students should have similar accountability for each.

Third, both students and teachers must be educated that assaulting a teacher will bring swift consequences and that reporting assaults will neither diminish the teacher's reputation nor cost the teacher his or her job. Consequences must be realized in action and not just in word.

Sometimes the most loving thing a parent, teacher, and school can do can be the hardest thing imaginable: holding a child accountable for behaviors that injure others. No one wants to believe his or her child hit a teacher. However, the message needs to be sent that violence against teachers is never to be tolerated.

Fourth, teaching is not a contact sport, where physical touching and roughness are part of the game called education. A quick search of Internet videos might yield a different conclusion. Students and parents can be seen cheering when violence occurs against teachers. This demonstrates how low our culture has sunk.

Education is not a game and school is not a stadium. Violence against teachers needs to be called out. Recordings of teachers being assaulted at schools are nonconsensual, and anyone taking or sharing them should be held accountable by the law and the school.

Laws need to catch up with technology, especially when safety is at stake. Absent changes in culture and law, students will continue to practice what incites viral madness. Each time such videos are shared and viewed, it is as if the assault takes place for the first time, all over again.

NOTES

1. Tim Walker. "Violence against teachers—an overlooked crisis?" *NEA Today*. February 19, 2014. Retrieved from http://neatoday.org/2013/02/19/violence-against-teachers-an-overlooked-crisis-2/.

2. Michael D. Simpson. "What NEA affiliates are doing to protect members from violent and disruptive students." July 12, 2017. *National Education Association*. Retrieved from www.nea.org/archive/42238.htm.

3. Ibid.

4. James Walsh. "St. Paul teachers threaten strike over school violence." December 10, 2015. *The Star Tribune*. Retrieved from www.startribune.com/silva-to-address-questions-of-teacher-safety-and-union-s-request-for-mediation/361318431/.

5. Anthony Lonetree. "Teacher injured in Central High attack was at fault, district alleges." *The Star Tribune*. April 1, 2016. Retrieved from www.startribune.com/teacher-injured-in-central-high-attack-was-at-fault-district-alleges/374194681/.

6. Josh Verges. "St. Paul teacher's lawsuit over Central High assault dismissed." *Twin Cities Pioneer Press*. May 25, 2017. Retrieved from www.twincities.com/2017/05/25/ekblad-judge-dismisses-st-paul-teachers-lawsuit-over-central-high-assault/.

7. Linda Conner Lambeck. "Teachers learning to file assault complaints." *Connecticut Post*. July 22, 2012. Retrieved from http://archive.boston.com/news/education/articles/2012/07/22/teachers_learning_to_file_assault_complaints/.

8. Rowena Coetsee. "Antioch: 13-year-old girl cited for beating middle-school teacher." *Mercury News*. February 4, 2017. Retrieved from www.mercurynews.com/2017/02/02/antioch-punishing-students-for-big-offenses-can-be-complicated/.

9. Ibid.

10. Ibid.

11. Ibid.

12. Ernest J. Zarra III. *Helping parents understand the minds and hearts of Generation Z.* 2017. Lanham, MD: Rowman & Littlefield, pp. 5–8. Italics added by author.

13. Parent interview with this author. August 24, 2017.

14. George Brown. "Attack on Wooddale teacher caught on video." *WREG*. May 18, 2016. Retrieved from http://wreg.com/2016/05/18/teacher-attacked-at-wooddale-high-school/.

15. Joel Hood. "Teachers attacked by students show signs of post-traumatic stress disorder." *Chicago Tribune*. July 2, 2012. Retrieved from http://articles.chicagotribune.com/2012-07-02/news/ct-met-teacher-assault-20120702_1_ptsd-stress-disorder-chicago-public-schools-teacher.

16. Ibid.

17. Staff. "Police: Student assaulted BHS teacher, faces felony charge." *Burleson Star*. November 9, 2016. Retrieved from www.burlesonstar.net/news/police-student-assaulted-bhs-teacher-faces-felony-charge. Cf. Liz Farmer. "Burleson student faces felony charge for shoving teacher into doorknob, police say." *The Dallas Morning News*. November 10, 2016. Retrieved from www.dallasnews.com/news/crime/2016/11/10/burleson-student-faces-felony-charge-shoving-teacher-doorknob-police-say.

18. Jovana Lara. "John Muir teacher attacked by parent, daughters speak out—exclusive." *ABC Eyewitness News*. March 6, 2014. Retrieved from http://abc7.com/archive/9021330/.

19. Don Matics. "Admins: Teachers to blame for student assault." *FOX 13 NEWS*. April 28, 2017. Retrieved from www.fox13news.com/news/local-news/251513737-story.

20. Ibid.

21. Ibid.

22. Ibid.

23. "Teachers in the Word." *Facebook Group*. October 4, 2017. Retrieved from www.facebook.com/groups/teachersintheword/.

24. Rudy Miller. "'Interventionist team' sent to Easton school to quell bad behavior." *LehighValleyLive*. May 23, 2017. Retrieved from www.lehighvalleylive.com/easton/index.ssf/2017/05/interventionist_team_sent_to_e.html.

25. Hans Bader. "Obama Administration undermines school safety, pressures schools to adopt racial quotas in student discipline." *Competitive Enterprise Institute*. January 13, 2014.

Retrieved from https://cei.org/blog/obama-administration-undermines-school-safety-pressures-schools-adopt-racial-quotas-student. Cf. *United States, Petitioner v. Christopher Lee Armstrong*. Supreme Court of the United States. May 13, 1996. Retrieved from www.law.cornell.edu/supct/html/95-157.ZO.html.

26. Mark Keierleber. "Is DeVos near ending school discipline reform after talks on race, safety?" *The 74*. November 20, 2017. Retrieved from www.the74million.org/article/is-devos-near-ending-school-discipline-reform-after-talks-on-race-safety/.

27. Ibid.

28. Mark Meckler. "College has 'White people-free day' on campus: Chaos ensues." *Patheos*. June 4, 2017. Retrieved from www.patheos.com/blogs/markmeckler/2017/06/college-white-people-free-day-campus-chaos-ensues/.

29. Ibid.

30. Ibid.

31. Walter E. Williams. "The ugly facts about student violence against teachers." *Be the People*. September 16, 2015. Retrieved from www.bethepeopletv.com/the-ugly-facts-about-student-violence-against-teachers/.

32. Carrie Dann. "NBC/WSJ Poll: Americans pessimistic on race relations." *NBC NEWS*. September 21, 2017. Retrieved from www.nbcnews.com/politics/first-read/nbc-wsj-poll-americans-pessimistic-race-relations-n803446?cid=sm_npd_nn_tw_ma.

33. Simon Heffer. "How eight years of Barack Obama created Donald Trump." *The Telegraph*. January 20, 2017. Retrieved from www.telegraph.co.uk/news/2016/11/09/how-eight-years-of-barack-obama-created-donald-trump/.

34. Amanda Marcotte. "New election analysis: Yes, it really was blatant racism that gave us President Donald Trump." *Salon*. April 9, 2017. Retrieved from www.salon.com/2017/04/19/new-election-analysis-yes-it-really-was-blatant-racism-that-gave-us-president-donald-trump/.

35. Laurie Futterman. "Beyond the classroom: The impact of culture on the classroom." *Miami Herald*. September 29, 2015. Retrieved from www.miamiherald.com/news/local/community/miami-dade/community-voices/article36727782.html.

36. Tyler Durden. "Middlebury professor assaulted, injured while escorting conservative speaker." *Zero Hedge*. March 3, 2017. Retrieved from www.zerohedge.com/news/2017-03-03/middlebury-professor-assaulted-injured-while-escorting-conservative-speaker.

37. Steve Reilly. "How to look up the background of teachers in every state." *USA Today*. February 13, 2016. Retrieved from www.usatoday.com/story/news/2016/02/13/state-teacher-background-lookup-resources/80355350/.

38. Jane Meredith Adams. "Most teachers in California say they need more training in alternatives to suspensions, survey says." *EdSource*. May 7, 2017. Retrieved from https://edsource.org/2017/most-teachers-in-california-say-they-need-more-training-in-alternatives-to-suspensions-survey-finds/581195.

39. Ibid.

40. Ibid.

41. Ibid.

42. Ernest J. Zarra III. *Helping parents understand the minds and hearts of Generation Z*.

Chapter Four

Violence against Teachers

School violence in general and its aftermath continue to be significant problems for students, teachers, staff, and schools. Most scholars agree that school violence is a multi-systemic problem.[1]

How common is violence against teachers in the United States and abroad? Is this only an American issue?[2] Here in the United States rates of violence against teachers are skyrocketing at an alarming rate,[3] but American teachers are not alone. Violence is plaguing schools all around the world,[4] and teachers at all levels are caught in the middle.[5] Oddly, teachers in the United States have their hands tied, almost daring students to make the first move.

TODAY'S STUDENTS

Violent students do not belong in schools. As part of the multisystemic problem, American culture appears coarser, and people are more prone to outbursts in public. Society seems less civil. Profanities are used as if there is something virtuous to interspersing F-bombs as conjunctions.

There is the perception today that, particularly in urban areas—and specifically embedded in some inner-city schools—places of learning have become places of refuge for the troubled. Some schools are hotbeds of social justice for others, and even food courts and halfway houses, for still others. Today's students are very much coddled, and they are the center of the education universe. Therein lies a main difference and it's generational.

Understanding the Differences

Students in Generation Z are very different than students of the Millennial or Generation X students of the past. Students today feel they are much more entitled, and some of this entitlement mentality is the result of schools perpetuating the notion that today's students are centers of their own universes. Some of this entitlement literally comes from states providing entitlement programs. Once an entitlement culture is established and a generation comes to rely on the entitlement, it is next to impossible to discard it or even reform it.

Gen Z practice their entitlements conspicuously. They do so by expressions of attitude and expectations and their uses of material goods and pursuits of leisure. One excellent example of this entitlement mentality is the use of cell phones. Gen Z feel entitled to use them as they wish in classrooms in ways to expedite assignments and as tools of social media popularity. There are issues with violence associated with students and their cell phones. The Internet is replete with evidence.

Today's students understand that laws and policies in schools seem to protect certain groups of students over others. For example, some students who would have been expelled just a few years ago for their actions now see Gen Z students' similar actions and that they are dealt with much more tolerantly. Previous generations balk at the multiple chances to return to school after wrongdoing. In situations like these, punitive justice has given way to restorative justice, and not everyone is thrilled with this change.

Restorative justice gives troubled and problem students many opportunities to get things right. Opportunities are good things. Applications of these opportunities cannot run counter to common sense. There are some successes, and these successes do come with a cost. One of the major problems, as well as an unintended consequence of the practice of restorative justice on the entitled generation, is its application of multiple opportunities that far surpass the realities of life. Once students leave the *just* confines of schools, life is *just* very different. Yet in so many cases, the expectations remain ingrained.

INCREASES IN VIOLENCE AND INJURIES IN CLASSROOMS

While any number of American schools may be declared as *safe schools*, the reports and anecdotes from teachers show otherwise. How can this be? Either administrators overlook circumstances that prove otherwise, or the definition of violence has been watered down to avoid having to report assaults and violence.

Teachers who are assaulted run the risk of being transferred or even dismissed for reporting incidents. On more than one occasion, teachers have been blamed for initiating the violent behaviors toward them. As the reasoning goes, there must be something in the environment of the classroom, the personality of the teacher, or students in the class that the teacher is not able to manage that triggers violence. So to district administrators and state bureaucrats, no reports of violence equals safer schools.

CHANGE AS A CONSTANT

Change is a constant in education. Teachers are forced to change things every day. Many of these changes run the gamut of lesson techniques and program and curriculum accommodations down to differentiated instruction. They even include behavior modifications. But teachers are also creatures of habit and routine, and students used to be much happier about operating in such routines. Often, they are quick to point out any divergence from their expected norm. Today, teachers are thrust in the middle of *habitual change*, often not of their own doing and usually irrelevant to academics.

Some change is unnecessary in education. Other change is imperative. There is no disputing these facts. When it comes to teachers, change often means the addition of another certification or the requirement of an additional credential. Change also means the introduction of another group of students of the same age level of a year before or adoption of new curricula, with new methods and correlated assessments.

What needs to change in education philosophy is the ignorance associated with the lack of understanding that students of the same age all share similar ability levels. The ages of children today are far less the same indicators of ability level of just a few years back, especially in primary grades. Assessment scores should be the proviso of evidence anyone would ever need to support the conclusion that students of the same age are truly not the same. The addition of special needs and learning-disabled students only reinforces this conclusion and brings new challenges.

Veteran teachers are more apt to understand the *primary elements* and aspects of a teacher's daily job, making them a valuable resource for newer teachers. Being a newer teacher is a classroom management constraint of its own. Certainly, veteran teachers may also be among those more reluctant to change.

Considering their experiences and what they know has worked with previous students, routine approaches often do not consider the changes in families and in culture. Gen Z students are a great example of what takes place when there is a clash of routine and change.

VIOLENT STUDENTS: WHAT HAS CHANGED?

What is being observed in today's students is both exciting and frightening at the same time. The excitement comes from knowing that learners are still out there asking for the knowledge and understanding that others have sought along their educational journeys. The fear comes in the reality that among these students is a streak of violence that pervades their culture.

Students today attend schools with hundreds to thousands of hours of violence wired into their brains and emotions. Students also experience violence directed at them at home. Furthermore, students participate in reality-type violence by means of video games[6] and online competitions. Interestingly, neuroscientific studies are making the connections between violence and the wiring of the brains of children. These connections need to be taken very seriously.

Younger students tend to live in a play zone and expect that this play should continue into their classrooms. Yet there is more than play involved. For example, if a teacher confiscates a student's smartphone, the teacher runs the risk of battling not only for the student's phone but something more soulful. The teacher battles the student's dependency.

Teachers have taken to the Internet to try to get through to some parents. In 2011, "a story published by author and teacher Ron Clark, entitled 'What teachers really want to tell their parents,' looked at reasons why educators give up on their field."[7] Some of the reasons shared by teachers include:[8]

- Your child's teacher is not your enemy.
- All children learn in different ways and at different levels.
- Your child may be well behaved or polite at home, but at school, he or she may pick on, make fun of, or bully others.
- ADHD is not an excuse: It is an explanation.
- I am appalled at the way teachers are being forced to teach to testing.
- Teachers aren't babysitters and shouldn't be responsible for teaching morals and respect to your children.

Another issue is the mindset of gangs and scores of students with little or nothing to do during the summer months. An example of how pervasive this mindset has become is clearly observed in an incident at a gas station in Memphis, Tennessee. A young Black father escorts an elderly White woman to her car to avoid her being harassed and feeling unsafe amidst a group of high school–aged Black males. He is immediately attacked by dozens of young men who descend upon him, apparently because he assisted a White woman.[9]

This type of violence is increasing in our nation's towns and cities, flooding our schools and classrooms. Gangs of young people trolling the streets and hallways of schools are far too commonplace in America's urban areas. Teachers who mention this very notion run the risk of the wrath of social activists.

Parents are quick to accuse teachers of racism and bigotry. But is this the reason for the gangs and trolling? Physical violence is becoming status quo, over cell phones and homework. Gangs replace families and impart their values to members. There is the appearance that America's national culture has gone backward by the empowerment of factions over the oneness of ubiquitous, commonly shared values. [10]

Family Is Paramount

Another very important thing that has changed is the redefinition of the family unit. Families are now defined so very differently than just two decades ago. The basic and fundamental building block of any society is its family. Every culture and society understand this.

When the family is redefined, shattered, fractured, or replaced by alternatives, there are ripples outward. Intensification occurs, and people call for government to establish and protect new norms. Children who are uncertain of their home lives or personal safety or who have experienced the horrors of family and community violence are deeply affected.

Children without fathers or mothers or whose parents have been incarcerated are also deeply affected. Gangs that swoop in to provide a family network for those confused, disaffected, and lonely outcasts also have psychological effects on children.

All of these factors are important for many reasons, not the least of which is these children then come to school and are expected to abide by an adult's rules and apparent unreasonable expectations. Family is paramount! Is there any wonder why some students act out? Schools are supposed to be safe places for students. But how about the same consideration for teachers?

THE AGE OF RAGE

Classroom rage is dangerous. Injuries requiring medical treatment are on the rise. Does anyone question the numbers of injuries occurring but with so few reports filed? Acts of violence from students are more than expressions of roughness or coarseness due to changes in culture. But why are students so brazen today? That is a question that is difficult to answer in the midst of scissors being thrown with great force in the direction of one's head.

In these instances, the first questions should not be "What caused him to do that in your class?" and "Did the objects hit you?" Rage is dangerous, and if behaviors such as these are left unchecked, then schools will become worse battle zones than they are already. Likewise, reports of violence that are not filed imply that there is nothing wrong.

Those with track records of violence should not be able to spend every school hour each day with those seeking academic excellence in a safe and secure environment of learning. The state of Wisconsin is taking steps to move toward ensuring this environment by introducing bills in their state legislature so that its students "who want to learn can do so"[11] safely.

There is an argument that students will face violence in the real world so they must learn to deal with this sometime. If that is true, then the ultimate purpose of education in America is many times lost for purposes other than education—hence, social and political purposes. Our nation might as well establish schools in hospitals and mental health facilities. Sarcasm aside, academic institutions should not be hospitals for the emotionally and mentally ill.

STUDENTS GONE WILD

In this age of ubiquitous recording devices and immediate gratification of online attention, students become viral sensations and popular for having been "first" to see and post something. There is nothing too bizarre for students to post. They post intimate sexual videos, videos of cheating in classrooms, and videos of teachers disciplining students. They even post teachers being assaulted. Students today use their technology and the Internet as their own personal reality programming.

A simple YouTube search of the phrase "teacher fights" yields a multitude of posted videos. From parents berating coaches and beating teachers—to students and teachers involved in classroom brawls—the Internet is brimming with such violence. Students seeking their own viral kingdom have gone wild. Teachers must be wary. In this viral kingdom, it is not uncommon for teachers to be provoked into losing their cool and responding to a student's taunts and succumb to a student's eventual assault.

Take for example the John F. Kennedy High School in Paterson, New Jersey. A sixty-two-year-old physics teacher was attacked by one of his students after having confiscated his cell phone. The teacher was "thrown to the ground by a sixteen-year-old student,"[12] and it was recorded by students on their smartphones. The student was charged with assault, which apparently is not uncommon for JFK High School. According to a retired teacher, Lee McNulty, the school is a "place filled with chaos where fights are common."[13]

QUICK FUSES AND LACK OF SELF-CONTROL

There seem to be quick fuses on the parts of people in general. In Philadelphia, Pennsylvania, a sixteen-year-old student was late to one of his classes, which prompted an argument between him and one of his teachers. The result of the argument was recorded by a student at the end of the period. "Fists were raised and the student threw the first punch."[14] Police were called, and the teacher told them he had tried to "call security from his classroom but was unable to get help, and had to get stitches after the fight."[15]

Even some kindergartners are joining in on the assaults on teachers. As an example, in 2015, a Pittsburgh, Pennsylvania, kindergarten student continued "to act out at a western Pennsylvania elementary school, despite efforts including a 'cooling off' space and extra staff hired to deal with unruly students who allegedly attacked at least 11 teachers."[16] The principal at the school had been placed on paid leave and "replaced in the wake of complaints that he didn't act to stop the incidents."[17]

Four teachers and the school librarian have since resigned from the Pittsburgh elementary school because of the increase in physical violence. This increase was due in part to some special needs students who were mainstreamed without adequate full-time aides.

Students in schools across America have grabbed teachers' necks; kicked, bitten, and scratched them; and thrown objects at them in anger. The incidents described at the Pittsburgh elementary school are not an exception. Today's kindergarten teachers have to "constantly worry about their safety."[18]

On the brighter side, teachers in Allentown, Pennsylvania, agreed to a new contract with the Allentown School District. The new contract "protects teachers who have been assaulted by students."[19] In addition to raising salaries for teachers, the contract contains "a unique assault protection provision that provides association members protection from students who have assaulted them."[20] This is a good first step.

A few of the options in the contract to protect teachers include the provision that "a teacher who's assaulted cannot be asked to teach that student in a classroom or supervise them in another capacity." However, this does not apply to "encounters in hallways, cafeterias, bus duties or other general supervision over large groups of students."[21]

There are many questions that must be asked and answered. Some of these questions are both difficult to ask and probably even more difficult to answer. One roadblock to addressing both are the roles that bureaucracy and politics play in any given state. The fact is that some state policies might actually lead to increases in assaults.[22]

EXAMPLES OF TEACHERS UNDER SIEGE

The following media headlines tell the stories:

- "NYC teacher claims she was attacked by neglectful mom because investigators revealed her name."[23]
- "Parent's attack on elementary school teacher caught on camera."[24]
- "Mother is cited after teacher is assaulted at Truman Elementary School."[25]
- "Annika McKenzie, mom charged in teacher's beating, convicted."[26]

Additional examples are summarized in excerpts listed below. These statements are samples taken from lists compiled from several sources, including brief "snap online surveys" written and distributed by this author over the course of two years, online Reddit and sub-Reddit postings, and face-to-face contact with teachers as well as from personal emails, phone and personal interviews, and postings taken from several social media platforms set up by this author.

The educators' responses are representative of all levels, from K–16, and largely from public schools in the United States. Several college professors have also weighed in. What ideologies and beliefs lie at the root of these incidents?

- "My arm was purposefully jammed in a closing door by a student who knew I was exiting the classroom."
- "Male staff member had to deflect a punch, which was meant for a colleague's head. Student was allowed back into class after just two days. Immediately told the teachers to 'F-off.'"
- "Student in grade 2 placed thumbtacks on my chair, which I eventually sat on."
- "Threatened quite a few times and told by a student 'my dad is going to kill you.'"
- "I have been relatively lucky. But I have been kicked by a first-grade student and had a chair thrown at me. Also been told to 'F-off, you big ugly F.'"
- "Parents got angry and had tantrum during a meeting. They became livid and threw chairs around room."
- "I have been threatened many, many times. Also, a sixteen-year-old boy threatened to rape a colleague's baby. He was not expelled."
- "A colleague in a primary grade had a chair thrown at him and a table shoved into him and been purposely tripped while walking around his classroom."

- "Nothing was done when administrator was informed, after a boy regularly brought a knife to school in his backpack. A pregnant teacher took the knife from his bag and called home only to be yelled at."
- "Been told to 'F-off.' Things have been thrown at me by students. Some of my students are learning disabled and have serious mental disorders. Other students who have thrown things at me are reported to have horrible home lives."
- "Been screamed at by parents. The mother of one student was a regular screamer."
- "Attacked by a huge, terrifying mother. I had asked her son to stop behaving a certain way. She screamed at me over my disallowing her child to do what he wanted while in class."
- "I was threatened by a dad with physical violence because I reprimanded his son in class."
- "My teacher's aide was badly injured after intervening in a fight between two fifth-grade boys. She was told she should not have gotten involved and it was implied it was her fault for getting injured."
- "My accent was made fun of by sixth graders and belittled when they were caught whispering 'mofo' to each other."
- "One of my sixth graders stole my coat."
- "Reported an assault to my administrators, and my report was undermined by colleagues, who claimed I was partly at fault."

For the purpose of this book, a more extensive and wider-reaching national survey was conducted, the data collected, and the results analyzed. See appendix 1 for the complete survey and comprehensive data. Select highlights of the survey will be included later in this chapter.

CULTURAL CLASHES

Some teachers who identify themselves as LBGTQ have become activists in class. They perceive they are under attack by religious groups in society and in some schools. Sometimes, they feel as if their values and identities are being assaulted. This perception carries over and sometimes affects students.

One example of these effects occurred when a lesbian teacher asked students to remove the crosses they were wearing on their necks because of the feeling the crosses gave her. She believed the crosses gave the impression that students who wore them were anti-gay and part of a "gang" that was anti-LGBTQ. Meanwhile, the teacher's partner, who also works at the same school, "dressed up as a nun for the school's spirit week—with a cross composed of small skulls."[27]

When teachers' beliefs are assaulted and collide with students' beliefs, what is a society to do? What is a society to do when students' beliefs feel threatened by a person with authority pressuring them toward a viewpoint in which they sense discomfort? Is violence the answer? Is provocation by teachers an acceptable expression, and is a public school classroom the appropriate forum?

In the case just mentioned, should a person's sexuality take precedence over others' religious expression? Furthermore, what happens when a person's religious expression has to give way to others' personal sexual and gender expressions? Heightened emotions already exist in today's classrooms. Any provocation by teachers might be used as an excuse for assaults to occur.

Some teachers do not want to have the added pressure of their lifestyles being challenged while at work. Others question how long it will be before these types of cultural clashes become violent. Due to the unwillingness of students and their families to accept what they view as activism toward alternate lifestyles and social engineering away from their cultural and religious beliefs, such backlashes may not be long in the making.

Political Marginalization

The disappointment of no longer having President Barack Obama in the White House and the subsequent election of President Donald Trump seem to have added to the marginalization of Americans. Just a few days after the 2016 presidential election, various high school and college student groups joined protest factions at schools in certain cities across the United States. These protests were usually organized at high schools or colleges and grew from there.

One such protest in the San Francisco Bay Area was formed and "two teachers at College Park High School in Pleasant Hill were assaulted by students . . . during a protest over the election of Donald Trump as the next president of the United States."[28] About two hundred students from nearby high schools began marching onto the campus of College Park High School during classes and began as mostly a peaceful protest. Two teachers were assaulted by a couple of students from the group during the protest.[29]

Differences in Political Ideologies

A recent Pew Research Center study revealed what many had already known. "Republicans and Democrats offer starkly different assessments of the impact of several of the nations' leading institutions—including the news media, colleges and universities and churches and religious organizations."[30]

During the last two years of the Obama administration, the views of Republicans toward the effect of colleges had turned more negative.

This turn in viewpoint is likely correlated to the media coverage of empowerment of groups seeking prominent voices on campuses, the protests and violence over conservative speakers invited to campus, and a shift in the values of children attending colleges with a vast majority of liberal professors.

As recently as 2014–2015, "most Republicans and Republican-leaners held a positive view of the role of colleges and universities. . . . Today, for the first time on a question asked since 2010, a majority (58%) of Republicans say colleges and universities are having a negative effect on the way things are going in the country, while 36% say they have a positive impact."[31]

Intolerance of ideological differences sometimes yields flashes of violence against professors as well as K–12 teachers. Intolerance of political differences has empowered student actions, some of which result in violence, especially on college campuses. Resistance on college campuses has its genesis in beliefs.

In comparison to Republicans, "the ideological differences are less striking among Democrats. Wide majorities of both liberal Democrats (79%) and conservative and moderate Democrats (67%) say colleges have a positive impact. However, Democrats are more ideologically divided than are Republicans over the effect of churches and religious organizations."[32]

Is our nation now at a point where differences in beliefs and practice cause immediate violent reactions? Personal anecdotes indicate that anger and differences do not always find their balance in tolerance. Students coming out of college are entering the teaching ranks. There is both anticipation and fascination to observe the students' transitions from the protected halls of academe to the different world of student protection. Soon, Generation Z will be teaching itself.

PRECURSORS TO STUDENT VIOLENCE AT SCHOOL

Espelage and Reddy have compiled a set of possible precursors to violence against teachers. Such a list is not infallible, but it is definitely worth noting. First, a disclaimer must be presented. All students exhibiting these traits will not go on to commit violent acts with certainty. Maturity and positive life experiences sometimes alter even the most hardened of souls, which is why learning to manage a classroom is so much more than a program or a trick strategy. Teachers can help to change lives.

Students facing external pressures at certain times, during certain phases of their development, might be more inclined to lash out. Likewise, some students do not need any external motivation to commit acts of violence. Espelage and Reddy offer their set of possible precursors as a practical matter—all of which should serve as beneficial information for teachers.

Beware also that these precursors listed below, when coupled with social media and online activity, might trigger some highly emotional in-class disruptions. These circumstances, referred to as classroom environment situations, also "can trigger disruption and rage."[33]

- A breakup with boyfriend/girlfriend
- Death/suicide of a family member, friend, classmate, or community member
- Arrest of a parent or a caregiver
- Parent separation and/or divorce
- Public/peer humiliation
- Family member fighting in war
- Prejudice (homophobia, racism, bigotry)
- Physical factors (hunger, allergies, gastrointestinal issues, sleep deprivation)
- Exposure to violence, aggression, bullying, and/or gang conflict
- Abuse (physical, sexual, and emotional)
- Natural disasters
- Economic stress
- Strained relationship between teacher and student
- Academic stress
- Peer isolation or ostracizing

STUDENT ARRESTS

The numbers of students arrested for physically assaulting teachers are definitely not a good indicator of the problems of violence that exist in schools. There are a few reasons for this. First, the younger the student, the less likely there will be any report filed or arrest made. The example of the autistic student arrested recently made national headlines for the sake of empathy toward special needs students and for the fact that he was younger.

A second reason the number of arrests is not a good indicator of the severity of the problem is that each incident is handled separately. Therefore, even older students avoid major consequences due to special circumstances. Many students who assault teachers are not arrested, or a deal is struck to remove the student to another school. Apparently, the numbers of teachers with bruised shins, stab mark scars, and book and other object marks on their bodies are becoming part of the new undocumented group. It is apparent that becoming a teacher today brings with it the expectation of an acceptable risk of being injured—especially in the primary elementary grades.

A third reason the numbers of student arrests are underreported is a lack of support from administrators and principals. School administrators are both fearful of reporting increases of violence and woeful in their support of teachers who defend themselves against weak administrative efforts. Sometimes this pays off monetarily for injured teachers,[34] and such outcomes only add to the weaknesses of the administrators.

The optics do appear one-sided. Little bodies, a towering figure in class, and everyone wonders, how can this disparity result in a teacher being assaulted? Nevertheless, incidents that are not legally reported, do inflict pain and injury. Teachers have proven very tolerant of injuries inflicted upon them by students. This has to change. Social justice advocates should be upset. But this is not what some social activists have in mind when they reference *tolerance*.

INTERNATIONAL STUDENTS GONE WILD

Reddy and colleagues write: "Violence against teachers is a larger problem than many individuals realize . . . the prevalence of violence perpetrated against teachers is great . . . broad in scope, with the most common form of violence consisting of verbal assaults, followed by threats and physical attacks."[35] But assaults against teachers are not just an American problem.

Ireland

Violence with injuries—and even death—are being reported around the world. According to the Irish National Teachers Organization (INTO), there are serious problems with students "kicking, biting, screaming, shouting, throwing furniture and verbal threat in both mainstream and special primary and post-primary schools across Ireland."[36]

The INTO is so concerned about the students involved in the uptick of violence and in-class aggression that these concerns have caused teachers to come to work wearing protective gear. Once again, a correlating factor to violence is that "the children involved may have emotional difficulties, including autistic spectrum disorder, intellectual disability, ADHD, ADD, or oppositional defiance disorder, and some may be experiencing homelessness or serious family problems."[37]

Wales

In Wales, an average of "eight teachers are attacked by children every day."[38] The National Union of Teachers in the Cymru Region of Wales reported that teachers and other school staff members "have been the victims of more than 4,500 physical and verbal assaults by pupils," since 2015. Although numbers of assaults reported are slightly different, the Welsh government maintains "any form of violence or abuse against staff in our schools is unacceptable. We want our schools to be safe, welcoming environments where teachers can get on with their jobs, helping pupils achieve the best they can."[39]

Slovakia

In Slovakia, two studies were published in 2007 that addressed the problems and consequences correlated with teachers who had positive and negative *beliefs in a just world* (BJW). In the first study, researchers in investigating student violence against teachers in Slovakia secondary schools discovered that the well-being of teachers "can be explained by student violence and by a teacher's belief in a just world." Study number one "examined a representative sample of 364 teachers in one of the . . . Slovakian provinces, and found that 177 (49%) of them reported at least one experience of violence in the last 30 days."[40]

The second Slovakian study found that violence against teachers was "particularly widespread in vocational schools in the provincial capital."[41] One hundred eight vocational teachers "reported that they had experienced at least one act of violence against them in the last 15 days."[42]

The researchers concluded that levels of violence against teachers in both the regular public and vocational technical schools had correlational affects based on the teachers' beliefs in a just world. For example, "For victims of violence BJW was further associated with negative affect: the more they believed in a just world, the less frequently they experience the negative affect."[43]

The most interesting part of this study is that the absence of belief in values causes a vacuum whereby people are uncertain which direction to take or how to behave. One generation of people ignorant of their national values and traditions results in the next generation becoming less informed. Additional international examples of violence against teachers is included below.

- "Student assaults against WA teachers on rise." (Western Australia)[44]
- "Violence against teachers, employees alarms DepEd." (Philippines)[45]
- "Furious dad runs over teacher in front of kids after parking ban row." (Surrey, England)[46]
- "Break the taboo—Raise awareness for violence against teachers." (Germany)[47]
- "Govt announces new plan to end violence against teachers." (Australia)[48]
- "Violence against teachers a cause for concern." (Barbados)[49]

- "Mexican police unleash deadly violence against protesting teachers." (Mexico)[50]
- "Student violence against teachers." (Slovakia)[51]
- "Father who knocked female teacher unconscious in brutal revenge attack walks free." (London, England)[52]

PARENTS GONE WILD

What parents practice, their children emulate. Take for example the incident at the Pittsburgh King Pre–8 School, which has been described as "a rather shocking and violent incident."[53] A teacher at the school, Janice Watson, was enforcing a no cell phone school policy when she confiscated a cell phone from a fourth-grade girl. The girl bit the teacher, and her parents arrived at school and threatened the teacher and were "going to get even."[54]

On the way for medical treatment for the bite wound, the child's mother pulled up in a vehicle alongside the teacher's vehicle, which was stopped at an intersection. It was then the occupants of the mother's car threw a brick through the window of the teacher's car, breaking off one of her teeth and causing serious facial injuries. The mother was overheard telling the teacher, "I told you I would get you."[55] After all of this, the forty-six-year-old teacher was concerned for the student. She stated, "My heart goes out to the child, because what has that mother taught that child? Whatever it is, you solve it with violence."[56]

In another example, a student developed a kill list onto which teachers and students names were placed. One has to wonder why a student would develop such notions if his or her home life was stable and school was a place of nurture and safety. What is wrong with a culture that thinks this kind of behavior is merely child's play or a joke?[57]

Teachers as Targets

IES reports clearly illustrate there are several forms of violence that occur toward teachers. There is a tendency for people to lead with emotions and not rationality. The immediate gratification of emotion is supported by others online, which continues the emotional moment for hours and sometimes even until the next day.[58]

Martinez, McMahon, Espelage, et al. identified "individual and contextual factors" of 2,324 teachers and examined the correlates of "teachers who reported having been victimized at least once."[59] Their findings were quite revealing.

Male teachers were determined to be more likely *to report multiple experiences* of violence directed toward them. White teachers, both male and female, were "more likely *to experience multiple forms* of violence generated by students and parents."[60] Some additional findings of this 2016 study published in the *Journal of School Violence*[61] include:

- The researchers also concluded that when a teacher takes the blame upon her- or himself, that such attribution seems to lead to additional violent actions toward the teacher.
- Teachers who responded that there was little to no administrative support were more likely to experience additional violence against them.
- Teachers working in urban settings were more inclined to experience violence against them and to report multiple offenses.

WHAT NEEDS TO BE DONE

All students are not cut out for the regimen and rigors of seated academics. Programs should be modified greatly to reflect this reality. Games and fun technologies help students learn, particularly those with special needs. Students are often less likely to become violent with their ears budded and videos streaming—at least for the moment.

The nuclear family is being fractured, and students sometimes bring their reactions to family dissolutions with them to school. Schools cannot change the divorce rate or serve as clinics for opioid addicts. However, they surely can help students with some of the counseling that may be needed in efforts to understand why they might want to resort to violence themselves.

Since special needs students are now saturating public schools, genuine conversations should occur around whether mainstreamed students would better be served in specialized programs. Schools cannot replace families. Schools are constrained in that they cannot be the primary enforcer of behaviors. The students have to self-regulate and choose to be educated to their fullest potential.

Teachers and parents both desire children to learn how to care about others, share material items, and develop patience. However, some parents become incensed with schools that teach values that go against the values of the community at large or are deemed as being against their family or religious values. Some parents become abusive and even violent over the conflicts in terms of their deeply held beliefs.

Teachers view violence against them as a reason not to stay in teaching. Why would a teacher stay on the job if he or she experiences verbal assaults by parents? Who would endure coaching if parents question and berate the decisions made by the coach? As one colleague stated recently, "They don't pay me enough to put up with those things."

What are politicians and bureaucrats doing to alleviate some of the abusive online assaults that teachers may experience? This must be addressed.

The *bright flight* of teachers from the classrooms indicates there is a national trend, and it is of great concern. This phenomenon is examined and addressed in another book by this author titled *The Teacher Exodus: Reversing the Trend and Keeping Teachers in the Classroom.*

Teachers' reports of being bullied on the job are filling the in-boxes of administrators. This may partly be the result of looser laws opening the definitions of bullying, or more sensitive teachers, or a general coarseness in culture—all of which students are a part. Laws must be written to ensure protection for teachers.

These laws must be enforced, and students and parents must be held accountable for any assaults upon teachers. Schools have the right idea in protecting students, but they cannot stop there. A good start would be for teachers to receive targeted and practical professional development on how to respond to and deal with angry parents and violent students. [62]

The reality today is that teacher shortages are occurring all over America. One of the drivers of these shortages in states is the lack of support from administrators over disruptive and violent students. Private schools are thriving and so also are homeschools. Why are these models thriving? Public education is not what it used to be. The days of American educational excellence appear to be over.

Teaching in public education now involves so much more for the teacher, with so much less protection. Burnout is real, both physically and psychologically. It happens sooner than in other careers. School districts must be compelled to do more to assist teachers in fanning the flames of their passions for teaching and serving in their chosen careers. They can begin by getting serious about teacher assaults.

NOTES

1. Dorothy Espelage, Eric M. Anderman, Veda Evanell Brown, et al. "Understanding and preventing violence directed against teachers." *American Psychologist.* February–March 2013. Vol. 68, No. 2, pp. 75–87.

2. Tom Wills and Ami Sedghi. "How common is violence against a teacher?" *The Guardian.* April 25, 2014. Retrieved from www.theguardian.com/news/datablog/2014/apr/29/ann-maguire-stabbing-how-common-is-violence-against-a-teacher.

3. Lauretta Brown. "Student attacks on teachers up 34%; Record 209,800 in 2011–12 school year." *American Renaissance.* June 10, 2014. Retrieved from www.amren.com/news/2014/06/student-attacks-on-teachers-up-34-5-record-209800-in-2011-12-school-year/.

4. Staff. "Assaults on teachers: An introduction." *European Agency for Occupational Safety and Health.* December 2015. Retrieved from www.into.ie/ROI/InfoforTeachers/BehaviourandDiscipline/AssaultsOnTeachers/.

5. Elizabeth Behrman. "Classrooms in crisis: Violence plagues schools." *Trib Live.* January 10, 2016. Retrieved from http://triblive.com/news/education/9709262-74/students-teachers-teacher.

6. Jack Hollingdale and Tobias Greitemeyer. "The effect of online violent video games on levels of aggression." *PLOS One.* November 12, 2014. Retrieved from http://journals.plos.org/plosone/article?id=10.1371/journal.pone.0111790. Cf. Douglas A. Gentile, Paul J. Lynch, Jen-

nifer Ruh Linder, et al. "The effects of violent video game habits on adolescent hostility, aggressive behaviors, and school performance." *Journal of Adolescence.* February 2004. Vol. 27, No. 1, pp. 5–22. Retrieved from www.sciencedirect.com/science/article/pii/ S0140197103000927.

7. Ron Clark. "What teachers really want to tell parents." *CNN.* March 14, 2013. Retrieved from www.cnn.com/2011/09/06/living/teachers-want-to-tell-parents/index.html.

8. Nicole Saidi. "I'm not your enemy: 10 things parents and teachers want each other to know." *CNN.* March 14, 2013. Retrieved from www.cnn.com/2013/03/14/living/parents-teachers-10-things/index.html.

9. Staff. "Mob attacks man at Tennessee gas station after he helps old lady get to her car." *Patriot Chronicle.* July 17, 2017. Retrieved from http://article.patriotchronicle.com/mob-attacks-man-at-tennessee-gas-station-after-he-helps-old-lady-get-to-her-car-h/.

10. Jennifer Agiesta. "Under Obama, 4 in 10 say race relations worsened." *CNN Politics.* March 13, 2015. Retrieved from www.cnn.com/2015/03/06/politics/poll-obama-race-relations-worse/index.html.

11. Will Flanders and Natalie Goodnow. "Obama school discipline policies hurt Wisconsin kids." *Journal Sentinel.* November 27, 2017. Retrieved from www.jsonline.com/story/opinion/contributors/2017/11/27/obama-school-discipline-policies-hurt-wisconsin-kids/888583001/.

12. Jonathan Turley. "New Jersey teacher attacked in classroom after confiscating cell phone from student." *Res Ipsa Loquitur.* January 28, 2015. Retrieved from https://jonathanturley.org/2015/01/28/new-jersey-teacher-attacked-in-classroom-after-confiscating-cellphone-from-student/.

13. Staff. "Student arrested after classroom attack on NJ high school teacher caught on video." *FOXNEWS.* January 27, 2015. Retrieved from www.foxnews.com/us/2015/01/27/student-arrested-after-classroom-attack-on-nj-high-school-teacher-caught-on.html.

14. Staff. "Student charged with assault after fighting high school teacher." *NBC4.* September 21, 2016. Retrieved from http://nbc4i.com/2016/09/21/student-charged-with-assault-after-fighting-high-school-teacher/.

15. Ibid.

16. Staff. "Kindergarteners behind latest incidents at unruly Woodland Hills school." *WTAE-TV.* November 13, 2015. Retrieved from www.wtae.com/article/kindergartners-behind-latest-incidents-at-unruly-woodland-hills-school/7475144.

17. Ibid.

18. Ibid.

19. Sara Satullo. "Allentown teachers get higher pay, assault protections in new pact." *Lehigh Valley Live.* March 15, 2016. Retrieved from www.lehighvalleylive.com/allentown/index.ssf/2016/03/allentown_teachers_to_see_high.html.

20. Ibid.

21. Ibid.

22. Will Flanders and Natalie Goodnow. "Obama school discipline policies hurt Wisconsin kids." *Journal Sentinel.* November 27, 2017. Retrieved from www.jsonline.com/story/opinion/contributors/2017/11/27/obama-school-discipline-policies-hurt-wisconsin-kids/888583001/.

23. Victoria Bekiempis. "NYC teacher claims she was attacked by neglectful mom because investigators revealed her name." *New York Daily News.* November 22, 2016. Retrieved from www.nydailynews.com/new-york/manhattan/nyc-teacher-beaten-neglectful-mom-sues-investigators-article-1.2882868.

24. Kara Duffy. "Parent's attack on elementary school teacher caught on camera." *WCTV.* January 6, 2014. Retrieved from www.wctv.tv/home/headlines/Parent-Attacks-Teacher-Over-Visitors-Pass-206514261.html.

25. Christine Vendel and Tony Rizzo. "Mother is cited after teacher is assaulted at Truman Elementary School." *The Kansas City Star.* September 6, 2013. Retrieved from www.kansascity.com/news/local/article326837/Mother-is-cited-after-teacher-is-assaulted-at-Truman-Elementary-School.html.

26. Chau Lam. "Annika McKenzie, mom charged in teacher's beating, convicted." *Newsday.* January 12, 2017. Retrieved from www.newsday.com/long-island/nassau/annika-mckenzie-mom-charged-in-teacher-s-beating-convicted-1.12947474.

27. Dave Huber. "Complaint: Teacher made students remove Christian cross necklaces, called them gang symbols." *The College Fix.* April 22, 2017. Retrieved from www. thecollegefix.com/post/32238/.

28. Allison Weeks. "Two teachers assaulted during Anti-Trump protest in Pleasant Hill." *KRON News.* November 10, 2016. Retrieved from http://kron4.com/2016/11/10/two-teachers-assaulted-during-anti-trump-protest-in-pleasant-hill/.

29. Ibid.

30. Staff. "Sharp partisan divisions in views of national institutions." *Pew Research Center.* July 10, 2017. Retrieved from www.people-press.org/2017/07/10/sharp-partisan-divisions-in-views-of-national-institutions/.

31. Ibid.

32. Ibid.

33. Dorothy Espelage and Linda Reddy. "Understanding and preventing violence directed against teachers: Recommendations for a national research, practice and policy agenda: American Psychological Association Board of Educational Affairs Task Force on Classroom Violence Directed Against Teachers." *American Psychological Association.* 2016. Retrieved from www.apa.org/education/k12/teacher-victimization.pdf.

34. Dave Urbanski. "Teacher—allegedly told to 'put her big girl panties on' by principal—wins big settlement." *The Blaze.* July 27, 2017. Retrieved from http://www.theblaze.com/news/2017/07/27/teacher-allegedly-told-to-put-her-big-girl-panties-on-by-principal-wins-big-settlement.

35. Linda A. Reddy, Dorothy L. Espelage, Susan D. McMahon, et al. "Violence Against Teachers: Case Studies from the APA Task Force." *International Journal of School & Educational Psychology.* Vol. 1, No. 4, pp. 231-245 (viz. p. 242). December 4, 2013. Retrieved from http://www.tandfonline.com/doi/full/10.1080/21683603.2013.837019.

36. Peter McGuire. "Teachers wearing protective gear against assaults by pupils." *The Irish Times.* April 19, 2017. Retrieved fromwww.irishtimes.com/news/education/teachers-wearing-protective-gear-against-assaults-by-pupils-1.3054336.

37. Ibid.

38. Abbie Wightwick. "Eight teachers are attacked every day at schools in Wales." *Wales Online.* January 30, 2017. Retrieved fromwww.walesonline.co.uk/news/wales-news/eight-teachers-attacked-every-day-12526042.

39. Ibid.

40. Josef Dzuka and Claudia Dalbert. "Student violence against teachers." *European Psychologist.* No. 12, pp. 253–260. November 2007. Retrieved from http://econtent.hogrefe.com/doi/abs/10.1027/1016-9040.12.4.253.

41. Ibid.

42. Ibid.

43. Ibid.

44. Regina Titelius. "Student assaults against WA teachers on rise." *Perth Now.* January 7, 2017. Retrieved from www.perthnow.com.au/news/western-australia/student-assaults-against-wa-teachers-on-rise/news-story/0781ad322d8e0942b86fe308bbc5844b.

45. Janvic Mateo. "Violence against teachers, employees alarms DepEd." *The Philippine Star.* July 6, 2017. Retrieved from www.philstar.com/campus/education/2017/07/06/1716784/violence-against-teachers-employees-alarms-deped.

46. Editors. "Furious dad runs over teacher in front of kids after parking ban row." *The Sun.* September 25, 2017. Retrieved from www.thesun.co.uk/news/4543290/dramatic-moment-parent-runs-over-teacher-in-front-of-stunned-pupils-after-strict-heads-parking-ban/.

47. Education International. "Break the taboo—Raise awareness for violence against teachers." *Worlds of Education.* April 12, 2017. Retrieved from https://worldsofeducation.org/en/woe_homepage/woe_detail/14824/break-the-taboo-%E2%80%93-raise-awareness-for-violence-against-teachers.

48. James Reid. "Govt announces new plan to end violence against teachers." *The Educator.* July 27, 2017. Retrieved from www.educatoronline.com.au/news/govt-announces-new-plan-to-end-violence-against-teachers-239211.aspx. Cf. Stefanie Balogh and Sean Parnell. "Teacher bashings by 'angry parents' and students on the rise." *The Australian.* January 31, 2017.

Retrieved   from   www.theaustralian.com.au/national-affairs/education/teacher-bashings-by-angry-parents-and-students-on-the-rise/news-story/081cd9bd2c09f75774ee5f2245d77107.

49. Staff. "Violence against teachers a cause for concern." *The Barbados Advocate*. April 5, 2017. Retrieved from www.barbadosadvocate.com/news/violence-against-teachers-cause-concern.

50. Lauren McCauley. "Mexican police unleash deadly violence against protesting teachers." *Common Dreams*. June 20, 2016. Retrieved from www.commondreams.org/news/2016/06/20/mexican-police-unleash-deadly-violence-against-protesting-teachers.

51. Dzuka and Dalbert, "Student violence against teachers."

52. Matt Watts and Hannah Stubbs. "Father who knocked female teacher unconscious in brutal revenge attack walks free." *Evening Standard*. January 20, 2016. Retrieved from www.standard.co.uk/news/crime/father-who-knocked-female-teacher-unconscious-in-brutal-revenge-attack-walks-free-a3160906.html.

53. Marty Griffin. "Police: Teacher violently assaulted after school, hit with brick to face." *CBS Pittsburgh*. October 18, 2017. Retrieved from http://pittsburgh.cbslocal.com/2017/10/18/teacher-assault-north-side-school/.

54. Ibid.

55. Ibid.

56. Ibid.

57. Simon McCormack. "Student expelled after allegedly trying to grab 'hit list' out of teacher's hand." *Huffington Post*. September 27, 2013. Retrieved from www.huffingtonpost.com/2013/09/27/student-expelled-kill-list_n_3996650.html. Cf. Ashley Collman. "Sixth-grader charged after allegedly planning school shooting and drafting list of 40 students he fantasized killing." *Daily Mail*. September 9, 2017. Retrieved from www.dailymail.co.uk/news/article-2416417/Sixth-grader-charged-allegedly-planning-school-shooting-drafting-list-40-students-fantasized-killing.html.

58. Robers, Zhang, and Morgan, "Indicators of school crime and safety: 2014."

59. Andrew Martinez, Susan D. McMahon, Dorothy Espelage, et al. "Teachers' experiences with multiple victimization: Identifying demographic, cognitive, and contextual correlates. 2016. Vol. 15, No. 4, pp. 387–405.

60. Ibid.

61. Ibid.

62. Meghan Mathis. "How to respond to an angry message from a parent." *We Are Teachers*. January 30, 2017. Retrieved from www.weareteachers.com/respond-to-an-angry-message/.

Chapter Five

Mainstreaming Violence

Regardless of the reasons, schools should consider protecting their teachers from students who threaten, intimidate, bully, or actually attack teachers. It's quite the conundrum, however, if a child has a disability. At what point do schools or adults draw the line in the abuse toward teachers? Researchers state tight rules and expectations in schools to protect teachers, but we are a school. How do we decide, essentially, which is more important? The safety of a teacher, or the education of a child? [1]

To begin, it must be stated clearly. Twenty-first-century political correctness has brought about a blending of the terms *special needs* and *special education*. As most educators know, special needs students and special education students are not necessarily the same categories of students. It also must be made clear that students from both categories are being placed into regular education public school classrooms in greater numbers. The reality is that "special needs children do not always have learning disabilities. . . . These students fit into a number of categories. . . . A special needs child is often considered disabled in some way. . . . Some of them simply have needs that must be planned for and addressed within their learning environment. . . . Most common disabilities, seen in schools, fall under developmental concerns." [2]

SPECIAL NEEDS BRING SPECIAL NEEDS

Developmental concerns that diminish learning sometimes also affect students' behaviors and expressions as well as affective filters for self-control. However, the topic of children with special needs is too often addressed very delicately among educators. In some ways, this is understandable. Since mainstreaming vast numbers of special needs students is a relatively new

phenomenon, there is fear of causing offense. However, what it is also causing is various problems for which teachers are not trained.

Public disenchantment of this phenomenon has not yet been realized.
When the nation comes to this realization, the safety of all involved will
weigh prominently on the minds of educators, parents, and members of the
larger community.

Special Protections

Special needs students and students specifically placed in special education
programs are broadly protected by laws at both the state and federal levels.
Special protections rest in their favor. There are so many financial and other
resource investments in these programs that teacher-to-student ratios, classroom aides, technology access, and specialized training are often the envy of
regular classroom teachers. But these resources are diminishing as more and
more special needs student are placed into regular education classrooms.

More and more school districts are now requiring special needs and special education students to be included in regular education for larger seg-
ments of their school days. How does this work for the regular education
teachers, and how do special needs students adjust?

There is a sense that today's culture has become pervasively and overly
sensitive when dealing with students in the special categories. Knowing this
should result in the awareness that this book is not meant as an indictment on
special needs students, special education students, or any teachers of students
in any such programs.

Certainly, there is no slight intended toward the families of students in
these categories. Unfortunately, we live in a culture where even disclaimers
can be questioned as veiled triggers in the minds of some. These are not the
motivations of this author. Honest and caring conversations can benefit all
involved. The question really amounts to whether regular education classrooms are the best fit for special need students.

The acceptance of a teaching assignment with multiple special needs
students is an exceptional undertaking for a teacher. If a teacher is assigned a
class that does not have a special education designation yet has within the
walls of the classroom special education students, it is only *a matter of time
and triggers* before a serious incident arises. Teachers should be made as
ready as possible to deal with special needs children. Professional development should be part of training for any teacher with mainstreamed special
needs students.[3] Monitoring the triggers of behaviors or the buttons that can
be pushed throughout the day can be exhausting. If the teacher has an off
moment, an unsafe environment may be created.

Tempered Tolerance

Understanding and tolerance of students' disabilities or disorders—especially if there is a previous track record of violent outbursts or rage in a classroom—have to be tempered with teacher and student safety. Classroom management at this point is far beyond what they teach in credential classes. This is why districts around the nation are providing *safe schools training* and what to do in the case of violence in the classroom. Most of the training is exclusive and pertains uniquely to each school and district on-site professional development.

When a student crosses a behavioral line and either the teacher or students are assaulted, making efforts to understand the reasons should become secondary to the safety issues and the consequences associated with such an incident. Not recognizing this and not reinforcing consequences of behaviors send the wrong message to all other students and contradicts even the best of intentions and interventions.

Criticism and Frustration

As Americans, we must move forward to the point that any critique of one student demographic or pointing out of incidents involving another is somehow hateful or an indictment of all students. Teachers across the nation are experiencing serious concerns in public school classrooms. Teachers who retired just a decade ago would hardly recognize the learning environments of today's classrooms. Mainstreaming and inclusion programs have changed the education profession in so many ways, even prompting a new wave of early teacher retirements.

Criticism is an easy matter, especially when done from the outside. Self-criticism and internal analysis are always much more difficult. From inside, the facts are that special needs students who are mainstreamed are finding themselves increasingly frustrated. Some of the noncompliant behavioral outbursts and violence are the results of these frustrations. This newer classroom reality must be addressed for at least three reasons.

First, the problem of violence is escalating, and it is affecting the learning environment. As a result, the problem must be addressed without emotional fanfare. *Second*, the new expectations that come along with inclusion programs require that the American public school classroom teachers need more effective training to be equipped to deal with these modern issues. *Third*, solutions that place more special needs and special education students in regular classrooms are not the best solutions for all students.

These are politically correct Band-Aids but not educationally correct solutions. Educationally it is just too risky. These issues are addressed in this chapter and throughout sections of chapters 3 and 6.

Addressing the Problem

Teachers and educators struggle through their days and wrestle with some very serious student issues. As they wrestle through how best to organize their classrooms and lessons and meet the needs that are presented as "special," teachers often find a variety of approaches must accompany these efforts. This is particularly so at the elementary level. "These educators are able to use cognitive appropriate teacher resources, teacher worksheets, and lesson plans. These tools are patterned for children with developmental issues. Not all disabled children need special classes. And, not all of them are capable of completing such classes. Here is where individual treatment again becomes critical. Remedial classes may be all that is required for some children."[4]

Equipping the Teacher

One particular program that seeks to bridge teacher training and credentialing programs of regular education and special education is found at Montclair State University. "At Montclair State, students can receive a dual certification in special education and a subject-level or grade-level range. The school also offers a unique concentration in 'inclusive iSTeM,' which specifically prepares science, technology, engineering, and math teachers for inclusion classrooms. Students in the program receive a Master of Arts in Teaching, a certification in math or science, and are endorsed by the state as a teacher of students with disabilities."[5]

Jennifer Goeke, the professor and coordinator of the dual certification program at the university, contends that "the dual-certification program prepares teachers to be hired as either a general-education or special-education teacher and that they know how to perform both roles easily and effectively."[6] In contrast to this new certification program, New Jersey's numbers of teacher assaults by special needs students have risen sharply. Is there more than a correlation here? Regardless of the program or certification, is it not likely that placing students with behavioral issues in regular classrooms might well cause secondary concerns?[7]

Too Risky

At Overland Park, Kansas, an elementary level special education teacher was hospitalized due to injuries sustained as a result of working with children given to violent outbursts. Apparently, working with special education students poses a serious risk but one that comes with the territory. Many special education teachers claim possible violence and injury are "just the nature of the children"[8] they have in class.

However, one teacher, Mrs. Anderson, received more than expected injuries. She received serious injuries, including a "concussion, human bites, a knee injury, and a second head injury."[9] Anderson's husband was worried about his wife. Although being injured periodically had become accepted over her fifteen-year career, her injuries were compounded due to the multiple head injuries, leading to an emergency ambulance ride to the hospital. Injuries do add up and take their toll.

Special education students are placed within specialized programs to help them learn to cope, and these programs usually have high ratios of teachers and aides to students. There are extra-special skills and training required by the adults who spend their days working in such challenging educational environments. They understand that there is the possibility that physical injuries can occur and that this possibility comes with the classes they choose to teach. But why accept assaults and injuries as status quo? There is nothing heroic about saying someone was injured seriously in an attack while in the classroom.

The risk factors change when students like those of Mrs. Anderson begin to be placed for an hour or two in regular education programs that are not special education designation. The equation changes. The ratios change. Class sizes of thirty to forty and only one teacher per class can lead to very difficult adjustments for all. Frustrated students in specialized classes usually do not find solace in faster pacing and more rigorous environments.

MAINSTREAMING AND VIOLENCE IN CLASSROOMS

Doctors do not treat patients as if they are healthy and normal if all indications are that they are not. Coaches do not play athletes who are injured or start players diminished in their abilities and pretend the team is at its best. This is not good for the athlete, and neither is it good for the team. Parents rear their children individually, and each of them has a different set of skills and abilities. Why then do bureaucrats and educational culture jam students into classrooms where they fit only because of age?

Teachers who excite students within their areas of interest and skill sets are more apt to see decreases in the risks of violence. For some students, excitement and interest are not enough to prompt motivation. Place students in environments where their focus is matched by the focus of others, and watch the violence decrease. Everyone is fearful of lawsuits. What about lawsuits from parents whose children are not receiving a decent education because of outbursts and time spent on students with emotional and behavioral disorders? All things considered, teachers tolerate so many things.

Is it any wonder that homeschooling in America is exploding in popularity? Or what about private schools? These schools are seeing record enrollments. Public schools have lost so many students. Maybe it is time to cave and reclassify some public schools as schools for those with special needs or continuation schools and seek better results.

The Every Student Succeeds Act (ESSA) of 2015 returned the focus on education back to the state and local levels after many decades of much more federally led education. In fact, recent executive orders signed by President Trump have begun to erode federal oversight and even federal education funding to states. [10] If funds continue to be cut, one can only expect additional special needs and special education students to appear in seats in regular education classrooms.

Students are becoming less self-regulated and more prone to tantrums in schools. Swelling numbers of students with emotional and psychological issues are resulting in increases in violence and causing serious safety concerns for all. [11] However, "every child has the ability to learn, but the way children learn and how much knowledge they can absorb can vary considerably—especially for a child with special needs." [12] This is the crux of the debate: safety versus inclusion. Can we have both?

Can All Children Learn?

The obvious answer is yes. However, it must also be asked as to whether all students can be taught. This is where there is often an education disconnect. Firsthand understanding of several local cases involving special needs students assaulting their teachers was quite revealing.

Recently, a local school superintendent issued a declaration that all students in his district deserved an equal education. This is a refrain echoed by almost every administrator. It is reminiscent of the mantra of just a few years ago that *all children can learn*. The announcement was the commencement that special needs and some special education students would be more inclusive in regular education throughout the day.

What the administrators failed to announce, and subsequently failed to enforce, is that all students also deserve a safe educational experience—including specially designated students now included in regular education classrooms. Inclusion in schools means greater risks and sometimes an increase in violence, where students and teachers risk injury or even death. [13]

At the elementary level, more schools are doing away with full-time special education programs and the full-time classroom "shadow" aides. Due to political pressure and economics, the paradigm for special education has changed dramatically in many states. Yet what do our local districts do when students assault teachers, sometimes sending the teachers to medical care? The answer most often is to place the violent students directly back in the classroom, prepackaged with the justification of the philosophy that "even special needs students deserve an education." [14]

In conversations with dozens of local teachers, it has been discovered that these teachers have been kicked, punched, and stabbed and suffered wrist sprains and limb bruises, some with injuries so severe that ice bags were deployed for visible swelling. Sadly, these incidents are not isolated incidents. As mentioned earlier, this is only natural. Many principals want to portray their campuses as "safe schools," so official reports are not always drawn up. Understandably, anger levels are rising on campuses, and now not just among students.

INCLUSION AS EXCLUSION?

Those who would proclaim unfairness and inequitableness to isolate students with disabilities and place them in special schools are missing the point. Special needs students are not being serviced for the needs they have. Most often, they are placed in classrooms with teachers ill-prepared to handle their special circumstances and not enough time to instruct them as needed.

Inclusion programs are naturally exclusion programs. Others miss out due to the individual attention needed by special needs students. Bureaucrats need to sit in on classes to view firsthand the frustrations of students who are misplaced. Special needs students thrust into regular education are sometimes lashing out and causing injuries due to their frustrations.

Students with learning disabilities are receiving more than a fair share of educational resources and services. However, by expecting them to achieve in a regular classroom, students without learning disabilities or special needs are actually being shortchanged. The intensity of the focus on inclusiveness in public education tends to place more responsibility onto the regular classroom learner while teachers spend required minutes each day teaching those with special needs. Therefore, inclusiveness by virtue of its practice also yields an exclusiveness, most likely an unintended consequence of a policy not well thought out.

Modifications and Accommodations

Modifications and accommodations are daily and weekly requirements for special groups. Teachers must spend a certain number of minutes with those of one or another specially designated category of students. Other accommodations that are made actually chip away at the quality of education for those students not classified as special education. Worksheets, computer time, silent reading, and other work are assigned to students while the required minutes are met. There are far too many jobs to do and far too many groups that need attention in accomplishing these jobs. This is why it is clear to many that public education in our nation is in serious trouble.

Data are clear that this type of classroom environment is just one more reason that charter schools, private schools, and homeschools are growing exponentially in the United States. It is also another reason for teachers either leaving the profession early or retiring early to find other work.

Double Standard

While it is not politically correct to hold the viewpoint that all students mixed together by age groups is not the best approach for students, the truth is that it is reality. Empathy should cut both ways, and the regular students are also not receiving their fair share of educational services. To reiterate, inclusion programs lead to exclusion of others.

A simple examination of the lives of politicians and bureaucrats would probably yield that many of their own children are neither in public schools nor ever attended public schools. Yet they make decisions for those whose children are affected. Education has become the favorite child of those with ideological bents that argue against what is perceived as social unfairness. [15] Does our nation suffer from an inclusion delusion? Political sense is vastly different from common sense.

A National Inclusion Delusion?

The consensus among Americans is that our education system is broken and it is too big to succeed. Broken education systems do not change by themselves, and they do not fix themselves. Students with disabilities do not fix their disabilities. So placing them in a regular education classroom, where they are often frustrated, and hoping for the best is at least questionable and at most, delusional.

Certainly, students can overcome their learning issues and become effective and productive over time. However, can they do so within the parameters of our nation's current education system? Might they best be served in schools that focus specifically on the ways they learn, more time spent on those ways, and lower teacher-to-student ratios? Everyone in education should simply ask what is best for the students. Common sense should prevail, not lawsuits at every turn of disagreement.

EDUCATION OVERHAUL

Our education system needs to be overhauled. This overhaul cannot take place with the addition of more and more students with very serious learning and behavioral disabilities, unless the system provides a choice of full-time special needs schools. The overhaul decisions have to be driven by abilities, not disabilities.

Schools that focus on placing students into classes where they will struggle or lash out because of a lawsuit or a political party's gains are focusing on the disabilities of students.[16] Teachers truly focus on students' *abilities*, which is why teachers are increasingly more frustrated by distractions that diminish this focus.

The discussion on fairness is directly related to teachers' points of focus. If schools truly were able to focus on learning of all students and sought to place students where they would find success, then that would be the ideal. The political climate in the United States stymies this from becoming reality, which is why the system is broken. Piecemeal or crumb approach to educating our nation's children will never amount to any meaningful systemic educational health.[17]

One argument for school choice is that students and their families would have opportunities to place children into schools in their areas that focus directly on the learning styles that special needs and special education students require. Currently, most of these schools are private and require tuition. However, with the possibility of money following the student, parents might find an incentive to form or support schools of choice for special needs students. If not, then the good news is that schools for special needs children are found all over the United States.

SPECIALIZED SCHOOLING?

From coast to coast, many states have terrific schools for children with special needs and/or learning disabilities. The teachers and aides at these schools are specially educated and trained to meet the educational learning styles of the students. For example, New Jersey has a list of approved private schools for students with special needs and disabilities.[18]

California also has its own list of private schools, which includes many fine schools for students with special needs.[19] Other states also have lists of schools. Some of these schools are listed in Table 5.1, which is a sample of the various schools available in many states.[20]

Anytime a public educator brings up private education in reference to special needs students, he or she is met with reactions that range from disgust to relief. There is disgust that a teacher would be a sellout. There is relief that someone finally has the nerve to suggest a system that might work better for students with special needs.

If the reader thinks a public educator is castigated for a suggestion such as this, how about the idea that parents are able to use their own tax dollars to fund their own special needs children at these schools? It is an impossible task to expect that public education can be all things to all students. If education is about what is best for all students and the current system is broken, it is the only sensible conclusion to reach. So why are schools even trying to meet all students' needs?

Table 5.1.   List of Schools for Those with Special Needs

American School for the Deaf, West Hartford	Crater Lake School, Sprague River, OR	Guilford Day School, Greensboro	The Piedmont School, Inc., High Point, NC
Ann Arbor Academy, Ann Arbor, MI	Currey Ingram Academy, Nashville, TN	The Hadley School for the Blind, Winnetka, IL	The Porter School, Roswell, GA
The Academy at Swift River, Cummington, MA	Davidson School Elwyn, Inc., Philadelphia, PA	Harmony Heights School, Oyster Bay, NY	Red Top Meadows, Wilson, WY
Aspen Ranch, Loa, UT	Denver Academy, Denver, CO	The Hill Center, Durham, NC	The Schenck School, Atlanta, GA
Atlanta Speech School, Atlanta, GA	DePaul Institute, Pittsburgh, PA	Holden School, Boston, MA	The Siena School, Silver Spring, MD
The Bedford School, Fairburn, GA	Devereux Glenholme School, Washington, CT	The Howard School, Atlanta, GA	South Dakota School for the Deaf, Sioux Falls, SD
Beverly School for the Deaf, Beverly, MA	Dore Academy, Charlotte, NC	The Ivymount School, Rockville, MD	Stewart Home School, Frankfort, KY
Brehm Preparatory School, Inc., Carbondale, IL	Eagle Hill School, Greenwich, CT	The Kingsbury Center, Washington, DC	Stone Mountain School, Black Mountain, NC
Bridges Academy, Bend, OR	Eagle Hill School, Hardwick, MA	The Lab School of Washington, DC	Stonesoup School, Crescent City, FL
Bromley Brook School, Manchester, VT	Eagle Hill-Southport, Southport, CT	Landmark School, Prides Crossing, MA	Storm King School, Cornwall-on-Hudson, NY
Brush Ranch School, Tererro, NM	Elan School, Poland Spring, ME	Little Keswick School, Inc., Keswick, VA	The Summit School, Edgewater, MD
The Carroll School, Lincoln, MA	The Fenster School of Southern Arizona, Tucson, AZ	The Melmark Schools, Berwyn, PA and Woburn, MA	Sunshine Cottage School for Deaf Children, San Antonio, TX
CEDU Schools	The Fletcher School, Charlotte, NC	Model Secondary School for the Deaf, Northeast, DC	Three Springs, Inc., Huntsville, AL

Centreville School, Centreville, DE	The Forman School, Litchfield, CT	New Haven, Provo, UT	The Timber Ridge School, Winchester, VA
F.L. Chamberlain School, Middleborough, MA	The Foundation Schools, Rockville, MD	New Leaf Academy, Bend, OR	Triad Academy, Inc., Winston-Salem, NC
Chelsea School, Silver Spring, MD	The Frost Center, Rockville, MD	The New York Institute for Special Education, New York, NY	Turn About Ranch, Escalante, UT
Children's Institute for Learning Differences, Mercer Island, WA	Glenforest School, Cayce, SC	Oak Creek Ranch School, West Sedona, AZ	The Vanguard School, Lake Wales, FL
Churchill Center & School, Town & Country, MO	Greenhills School, Winston-Salem, NC	Oakland School, Keswick, VA	The Vermont Center for the Deaf and Hard-of-Hearing, Brattleboro, VT
Copper Canyon Academy, Lake Montezuma, AZ	The Gow School, South Wales, NY	Oakwood School, Annandale, VA	The Vincent Smith School, Port Washington, NY
The Cottage School, Roswell, GA	The Greenwood School, Putney, VT	Memphis School for the Oral Deaf, Germantown, TN	The Woodhall School, Bethlehem, CT
The Cotting School, Lexington, MA	Great Lakes Academy, Plano, TX	The Oxford Academy, Westbrook, CT	
Coutin School, Canoga Park, CA	Gretchen Everhart School, Tallahassee, FL	The Phelps School, Malvern, PA	

SCHOOLS AS HOSPITALS?

Schools must not become places for the disturbed or special needs hospitals for those needing treatment for disorders. Schools are places of academic achievement and not meant to provide cures for the medical, emotional, and mental health ills of society. No one is arguing that compassion for students is not highly important. Certainly, children are our national heritage. Yet when assessments and local testing show that our nation is slipping in education, schools and communities have to wonder whether we will ever catch up. If our schools focus on societal ills, will this focus continue to diminish academic achievement? The answer is clear and the evidence is convincing.

Sending the Wrong Message

Students and parents who get a pass because violence may be redefined as an incident, or accident, or an event that comes with the territory in education is inconsistent and sends the wrong message. Again, schools are not mental health hospitals, where outbursts and violence may be daily occurrences. They must never be places where those who are prone to violence may injure others and themselves. Students with mental health issues are not being served in public schools, plainly and simply.[21] So the question remains: *How much less should violence be tolerated?*

Where special needs students may have the propensity to show rougher behaviors or be emotionally disturbed or bipolar students may exhibit coarser language, stages of rage, and tantrums, one must first question whether these behaviors would be tolerated in any other publicly funded arena. For example, in terms of bipolar students, there may be a hyperanxiety before tests, or they may become "argumentative, or aggressive with teachers of friends . . . resulting in an inability to concentrate."[22] How does one manage several of these students in class?

For example, teachers with students suffering bipolar disorder (BP) are instructed to find a "safe zone" for the students. "Students who experience significant irritability or rage episodes . . . who have attention problems may benefit from preferential seating, frequent breaks, and organizational aids."[23] This is problematic for schools. Although not necessarily a daily occurrence for one student, others in the classroom may have off moments and contribute to the disruptions throughout the day.

Certainly, teachers and schools never want to be found to be turning their backs on the needy—and students who qualify as special needs. However, a serious conversation must take place to address whether public schools are the best places for most students with these special needs to be served.[24]

The facts remain, on the athletic fields, in the hospitals, in public libraries, in the office, on college campuses, or on the roads while driving, there are expectations of behavior. Rage, potential for violence, and erratic behaviors are not found in these expectations. If extracurricular involvement comes with standards, how about similar respect accorded to curriculars?

RECOURSE FOR TEACHERS

In Ohio, teachers do have some recourse if they are assaulted by students with special needs. An Ohio court "allowed a teacher to sue the parents of an autistic student who viciously attacked her because the parents knew about the student's violent tendencies, but failed to warn the teacher."[25]

There is security for teachers who know their students' psychological, medical, and physical needs in advance. Teachers who are kept in the dark are flying blindly into each day and the challenges that may come their way. To illustrate this importance, the following bulleted comments are those shared by teachers on the National Education Association website in response to an article titled "Violence Against Teachers—an Overlooked Crisis?"[26]

- "A colleague of mine with some twenty plus years of service to his community and a teacher was suddenly berated by a student with a series of obscenities and vulgar statements. After three days of 'in-school suspension,' the student was right back in the classroom with no other penalty."
- "Teachers are getting assaulted weekly in our building. Administration was told only to 'handle' the severe violent or drug offenses. . . . Kids say they will start fights so when the teachers break them up, the teachers will get jumped."
- "I [also] teach students with emotional and behavioral disorders and had a student break off my front tooth during an aggressive attack. It wasn't his fault. . . . I work 60 hour weeks and have little patience left for my own children. I am looking for a new job."
- "An administrator knowingly put a violent child in my classroom without the proper support systems in place. Also, no one was notified how difficult the child was. On the first day of school, this second grader dislocated an aide's shoulder and body-slammed me into the floor during a floor activity."
- "Why aren't administrators backing up teachers? This is a recipe for chaos and violence that appears to be escalating in our schools."
- "I think the biggest issue with this topic is how strong is your administration?"
- "Unfortunately, many districts sweep behavior problems and assaults of students and teachers under the rug. . . . districts still allow undiagnosed mentally ill kids put in regular classrooms. The new rule is not to suspend black children . . . no matter what color they are, violent students should be expelled for the safety of staff and students."
- "I would like to see this issue propelled to TOP PRIORITY above all others. . . . It is commonplace to blame the teacher's classroom management skills rather than address the behavior of the perpetrators, this making the evaluation system inept. Teachers new to the profession promptly and wisely leave."
- "My classroom was very diverse with usually over 50% non-American students. These foreign parents treated me with respect and supported me in their child's education. . . . A child will learn little academics if they are being taught by their parents to disrespect their teachers and that if they do not do well in school, we will blame it on others."

- "Two female students were yelling at each other in the locker room. I went into the locker room, and one girl continued to curse at me and threaten to beat the other girl, so I asked her to accompany me to the office. She walked through the door first, stopped, and then slammed the door on me. It hurt my head, neck, and shoulder."
- "My wife (a 16-year veteran teacher of inner-city schools) was administering a test when two eighth-grade special ed girls from another class invaded her classroom, threatened several students, forced their way back into the classroom twice after my wife managed to get them out of the room, broke the door, and then screamed profanities and threats that they were going to come back and beat my wife up. During the course of the confrontation, my wife paged administration three separate times . . . eventually the security guard showed up to drag away the girls. Administration didn't even ask my wife about the incident until hours later. At that point she was still visibly shaken and emotional about the incident, and the administrator simply told her that there's nothing that can be done because the district prohibits expelling special ed kids and the maximum suspension per school year is 10 days."
- "Teachers sacrifice their own time, money, and expertise only to be humiliated in the media, and in turn by parents, who place no value on their child's education. Respect for education and educators is the only chance children have to escape violent environments. . . . I experienced or witnessed three acts of violence against teachers, substitute teachers, and paraprofessionals. . . . Teachers are not trained in criminal justice; they are not trained in law enforcement."
- "I work with elementary kids with emotional and behavioral disorders (EBD). So it is a known factor when I step into the classroom that my students are likely to threaten and attempt to harm me when I do something, like enforce limits that they do not like."
- "As a former local union leader and past president, I have seen my share of administrators that bully teachers. It happens every day and someone needs to step up and bring this subject out in the open."
- "I was attacked by a female student. When I protected myself I was told it was unnecessary force and was asked to leave. A lot of parents today see their child as the perfect angel and that we educators are doing wrong."
- "I was punched in the face by an autistic female student, while trying to help her speak a word related to a lesson. No warning from either the para or classroom teacher that this girl had this tendency to hit when she's feeling pressured. Drove myself to the hospital. No one offered to do so. . . . Is it any wonder teachers get disgusted when no one from the system cares about the well-being of their staff?"

WHAT NEEDS TO BE DONE

The following eight suggestions include ideas pertinent to what needs to be done toward overhaul or reform of education. These ideas are chapter specific and pertain to special needs and special education students in regular education classrooms. Also, these ideas are meant as action points and are not meant as a comprehensive list of *how to*, by any means.

1. Reconsider the philosophy that many special needs and special education students do not need full-time specialized education to achieve their potential.
2. If students are mainstreamed, everyone should take the violence and assaults by special needs and special education students seriously and apply consequences.
3. Reform state and local district policies toward greater protections for teachers and students who share classrooms with special needs and special education students to promote safer learning environments for teaching and learning.
4. Examine the levels of teacher stress and psychological and emotional effects upon both teachers and students in classrooms. Schools mandated to practice semi- or full inclusion of special needs and special education students are now causing higher levels of stress upon teachers.
5. Parents should seek legal remedies to undo some of the unfair practices that place both regular education and special needs and special education students at a disadvantage. The more special needs students in a classroom, the less the regular education label applies.
6. Examine inclusion programs more carefully to determine who and what is excluded by them? Time committed to special needs and the learning disabled in a regular education class means less time for teacher instruction for others, both with special needs of their own and others.
7. Parents should fight for their tax dollars to establish special schools or pull-out programs that have highly trained teachers to assist in the learning of their special needs or special education students. Mainstreaming places undue stress on many students, especially those with anxiety and various emotional disorders.
8. Teacher education institutions should include additional training for teachers to manage classrooms that are mandated for mainstreaming and inclusion programs.

Certainly, standing up for education equity means standing up for families—all families, even those with mainstreamed special needs students who might very well be on the receiving end of the violence from one of their very own. However, the model and the methods are not, and should never be, according to a one-size-fits-all paradigm. Challenging this conclusion might best be viewed through the lens of Common Core. The question should be asked: *Did Common Core's advanced rigors add to or diminish the frustrations of all students, including those with special needs?*

The time has come for education professionals, bureaucrats, legislators, social service professionals, psychologists, politicians, and classrooms teachers to sit down and talk. Part of their conversations must address the question, *Are special needs students truly being served in our public schools, or do they need schools that specifically focus on their styles of learning and understand their disabilities professionally and practically?* They should be ready for the answers and provide choices for solutions.

NOTES

1. Tracie Happel. "Student violence against teachers." *The Educator's Room*. March 24, 2016. Retrieved from https://theeducatorsroom.com/student-violence-teachers/.

2. Staff. "Teaching students with special needs." *Teacher Vision*. July 10, 2017. Retrieved from www.teachervision.com/special-needs/teaching-students-special-needs.

3. Candice Evans. "Five ways to help students with special needs." *Special Needs*. No Date. Retrieved from www.specialneeds.com/activities/general-special-needs/five-ways-help-students-special-needs.

4. Staff. "Teaching students with special needs." *Teacher Vision*.

5. Jackie Mader. "How teacher training hinders special-needs students." *The Atlantic*. March 1, 2017. Retrieved from www.theatlantic.com/education/archive/2017/03/how-teacher-training-hinders-special-needs-students/518286/.

6. Ibid.

7. Noah Cohen. "Teacher in videotaped classroom attack too injured to return to school, union says." *New Jersey Online*. January 28, 2015. Retrieved from www.nj.com/passaic-county/index.ssf/2015/01/post_4.html.

8. Molly Balkenbush. "Blue Valley special education teacher's husband described her injuries from classroom assault." *FOX4KC*. April 17, 2017. Retrieved from http://fox4kc.com/2017/04/17/blue-valley-special-education-teachers-husband-describes-her-injuries-from-classroom-assault/.

9. Ibid.

10. S. A. Miller. "Trump to pull feds out of K-12 education." *The Washington Times*. April 26, 2017. Retrieved from www.washingtontimes.com/news/2017/apr/26/donald-trump-pull-feds-out-k-12-education/.

11. Staff. "Mainstreaming special education in the classroom." *Concordia University*. January 6, 2016. Retrieved from https://education.cu-portland.edu/blog/special-ed/mainstreaming-special-education-in-the-classroom/.

12. Ibid.

13. Allie Bidwell. "Report: School crime and violence rise." *U.S. News and World Report*. June 10, 2014. Retrieved from www.usnews.com/news/articles/2014/06/10/incidents-of-school-crime-and-violence-on-the-rise-for-students-and-teachers.

14. Marcela De Vivo. "How inclusion can benefit special needs children socially." *The Social Express*. May 21, 2013. Retrieved from http://thesocialexpress.com/how-inclusion-can-benefit-special-needs-children-socially/. Cf. Noah Mackert. "Special ed kids deserve a first-class education. Top charter networks must give it to them." *The 74*. October 23, 2017. Retrieved from www.the74million.org/article/special-ed-kids-deserve-a-first-class-education-top-

charter-networks-must-give-it-to-them/. Cf. also, Staff. "Child is disrupting my class—what can I do?" *The Wrightslaw Way*. July 7, 2010. Retrieved from www.wrightslaw.com/blog/child-is-disrupting-my-class-what-can-i-do/.

15. Ernest J. Zarra III. "Community voices: Hazards of mainstreaming special needs students." *The Bakersfield Californian*. April 24, 2017. Retrieved from http://www.bakersfield.com/opinion/community-voices-hazards-of-mainstreaming-special-needs-students/article_0a7ff54b-84a8-53c2-a784-a57924ff7f1b.html.

16. Ibid.

17. Ibid.

18. State of New Jersey Department of Education. "Approved schools for students with disabilities (in state)." No date. Retrieved from https://homeroom5.doe.state.nj.us/apssd/.

19. Choices for Learning. "Private schools: Special education." Retrieved from http://choices4learning.com/school-learning/k-12-education/private-schools-special-education/.

20. Robert Kennedy. "Special needs schools." *Private School Review*. August 22, 2017. Retrieved fromhttps://www.privateschoolreview.com/blog/special-needs-schools.

21. Kevin Mahnken. "The hidden mental health crisis in America's schools: Millions of kids are not receiving services they need." *The 74*. November 7, 2017. Retrieved from www.the74million.org/the-hidden-mental-health-crisis-in-americas-schools-millions-of-kids-not-receiving-services-they-need/.

22. J. Elizabeth Chesno Grier, Megan L. Wilkins, and Carolyn Ann Stirling Pender. "Bipolar disorder: Educational implications for secondary students." *National Association of School Psychologists*. April 2007 (viz. pp. 12–15). Retrieved from www.nasponline.org/Documents/Resources%20and%20Publications/Handouts/Families%20and%20Educators/bipolar.pdf.

23. Ibid.

24. Elizabeth Behrman. "Classrooms in crisis: Violence plagues schools." *Trib Live*. January 10, 2016. Retrieved from http://triblive.com/news/education/9709262-74/students-teachers-teacher.

25. Michael D. Simpson. "What NEA affiliates are doing to protect members from violent and disruptive students." *National Education Association*. July 12, 2017. Retrieved from www.nea.org/archive/42238.htm.

26. Tim Walker. "Violence against teachers—an overlooked crisis?" *NEA Today*. February 19, 2014. Retrieved from http://neatoday.org/2013/02/19/violence-against-teachers-an-overlooked-crisis-2/.

Chapter Six

Teachers Assaulting Students

When I saw that in the paper, when I saw how he was being wowed and praised as this wonderful exemplary teacher . . . it hurt and it made me angry because I knew the truth behind what he had done. [1]

The focus of this book began as a study of the violence against teachers and what needs to be done about it. The frightening number of assaults occurring by special needs students and those with behavioral and learning disorders is shocking. These incidents are bad enough. However, also emerging from the research was the unmistakable reality that an increasing number of teachers were also crossing all sorts of boundaries with students. As a result, another disturbing trend began to take shape itself: *teachers assaulting students.*

Initiation of violence by teachers is taking place in the forms of physical, verbal, and sexual assaults. In the years since the publication of the book *Teacher-Student Relationships: Crossing into the Emotional, Physical, and Sexual Realms*, the allegations and arrests of teachers assaulting students have become even more disturbing. The assaults *touch* all possible definitions and reach across all forms and types of education institutions.

This reality is not a rationale as to why students are assaulting teachers. The evidence is clear there exists more than one problem as such in education today. There are parallel problems, and in this age of social media, information, photos, and videos, these problems find their way into people's consciousness through the immediacy of online posting. Teachers are falling prey to this medium.

OUT-OF-CONTROL TEACHERS

There is no secret that teachers use sarcasm and snide remarks to gain an edge over groups of mouthy students, especially when working with teenagers. Often, humor is interjected into the mix, and both students and teachers enjoy the bantering and razzing. However, words today tend to escalate to actions more quickly and more violently. For example, as the reader will come to understand, there are reports of teachers losing their tempers in classrooms and acting in ways beyond reason.

The research suggests students are being assaulted for at least two reasons. First, some of the students involved in the assaults upon them have been accused of initiating the contact. Teachers then respond by getting physical. Second, sometimes teachers are the initiators of physical contact with the students because of poor temperament and lack of self-control.

These teachers have been placed in environments that from the beginning were not suited for their personalities or skill sets. How many teachers' careers might have been saved with advanced professional development and training as to what to expect from today's students? No one will ever know.

Teachers Resisting

Verbal and emotional abuse are becoming more problematic as teachers refuse to take any abuse directed toward them. Students are more brazen today and more verbally defiant. Teachers are beginning to fire back and stand up for themselves. Self-preservation aside, teachers are going about this the wrong way. No teacher should ever assault a student. Yet at the same time, no teacher should ever stand still and take a beating either. The problem is that both are occurring today, and there is a dearth of support extended to remedy the problems.

Recently, a teacher was accused of biting a special education student. At first read, this comes across as quite bizarre. A report filed indicated that the teacher was bitten twice by the special education student before biting back. [2] Again, there is no good reason for a teacher ever to assault a student.

Under the law there is no reason a teacher should use biting back as punishment or to teach a lesson as to how it feels to bite someone. In fact, there are no good reasons for teachers to ever allow students to frustrate them so deeply that they would resort to any acts of violence or even using words of anger or threats. To be fair, physical injuries do more than affect one's psychological sensitivities and emotions. Physical injury energizes a self-defense preservation mechanism. In the strongest terms possible, teachers allowing students the latitude to affect their emotions to such an extent that the students' exercise this type of control over them is a compromise that should never be mentioned in the same breath as the word *teacher*.

Mismatched

Some teachers work in horrible conditions and have to deal with tremendous problems in their classes. Others do not work in conditions quite as poor. However, on any given day, most could admit to having had those classes that brought out the worst part of a teacher's humanity. In public education, teachers experience the real world before their eyes, in all of its rawness and crudeness. Given this, the education communities must face facts about themselves.

Some adults are not meant to work in today's schools with today's Gen Z students. They probably should have chosen another line of work, or at least a different content area, another school, or alternate grade level. Someone is falling short on the monitoring of the match between teachers and students. In a short period of time, the personalities of these mismatched teachers begin to emerge. What emerges is not often comfortable to realize.

Adults, like students, have bad days. A bad day is one thing, but being highly mismatched for work in today's schools is another. The fact is that even the best of trained teachers may not have the prerequisite attitude or skill set to handle classes.[3] Then, there is another issue: *the substitute teacher*.

The sheer number of substitutes filling America's classrooms across the nation should signal to American parents that some things are not working as they should. The natural deduction would be to conclude there are just more students than the supply of teachers. This reasoning does not address the question as to why there are fewer future teachers in the pipeline.

Certainly, not all the assaults are occurring with substitute teachers who cannot take the pressures of challenging students and classes overloaded with behavior problems. Veteran teachers are stepping over the edge more frequently. Students know those teachers who are serious and qualified in their craft and those who are not. Students are also good at deducing those teachers who could be *about to lose it* on any given day and what causes these teachers to *go off*. In all candor, some people are placed in situations that are tinderboxes, and some days, the incendiaries are sizzling feverishly as they enter the classroom.

Throughout nearly forty years as an educator, this author has witnessed temper tantrums from junior high and high school teachers. Witnessed also was swearing, throwing of chairs and hurling classroom implements at students, and breaking classroom technology as well as physically lifting students out of chairs and tossing them outside of classrooms.

In each of these cases, the teachers were neither officially reprimanded nor removed from their classrooms. These were obvious assaults that were hushed and dealt with privately by principals. Teachers with these types of temperaments are not suited to work with children, yet they are generally protected by their teachers' unions or associations. The problems have not gone away. In fact, there are good reasons to believe the problems have gotten worse.

TEACHERS SEXUALLY ASSAULTING STUDENTS

Teachers have been found guilty of perpetrating sexual assaults upon students. Both male and female teachers have committed sexual crimes with students, and these crimes have involved students from elementary school through high school. Recent examples of inappropriate and illegal sexual assaults upon students are included in the following section.

Sexual Assaults

On a larger scale, sexual crimes against children appear to be on the increase. To understand why would require a complete top-to-bottom analysis of the decades of changes wrought within the context of American culture. Social media and technology have changed the imagery of sexuality and pursuit of sexual activity. The recent "#MeToo"[4] social media hashtag was meant to highlight sexual assaults upon women and girls in the United States.[5]

At the time of this writing, it seems the world of immorality has caught up with the entertainment and political elites of this nation.[6] Therein lies a residual, leading to some students being assaulted. Culture is permissive and sexualized. Sexual assaults are also politicized. Double standards regarding sex exist in almost every corner of American culture.

In the state of Massachusetts, "Nearly one-third of the 774 investigations launched by the Department of Elementary and Secondary Education since 2012 involved educators who potentially crossed boundaries with children or adults in areas including sex, pornography, or intimate touching. Sexual misconduct is considered to be among the most serious transgressions by educators against students."[7] Add to this other forms of abuse, and matters go from bad to worse.

At the prestigious and private Marlborough School in Hancock Park, Los Angeles,

> In the early 2000s . . . former English teacher Joseph Thomas Koetters singled Chelsea Burkett out in class and made her feel special and independent . . . he gradually pulled her in and convinced her that she was in love with him, and that they were in an adult relationship. The contacts built from emails to sexual acts outside school. She was 16. When Burkett discovered she was pregnant . . . Koetters—who was married with children—tried to convince her to have an abortion. Burkett said she became depressed and bulimic and miscarried. . . . In 2015, Koetters was sentenced to a year in jail on charges that he had engaged in sex acts with Burkett and another 16-year-old girl.[8]

Table 6.1 includes examples of five teachers recently arrested and/or convicted for sexual assaults upon students. There are literally thousands of teachers who have been arrested in the past five years for sexually assaulting children, ranging from teachers in elementary schools through high schools.[9] In 2017, a former Portland, Oregon, teacher was "found guilty of sexually abusing six girls while working as a substitute gym teacher."[10] The odd part of this is that the teacher, Norman Scott, had received several previous reprimands for "inappropriate conduct" involving students from 2012, and he was still allowed access to students.

Sexual assaults are not only happening in public schools in America. In 2015, Jennifer McLeod was substitute teaching at Indiana's Hebron Christian Academy. McLeod, age thirty-four, was arrested after she kissed a seventeen-year-old student several times, at her home and at school, and after sending him flirty text messages. Part of the allegations included a text message wishing the boy was eighteen years old, "so they could have sex."[11]

Along with public and private schools' sexual assaults, there is also an increase of college professors being accused of sexual assaults of students. However, given the U.S. Department of Education's 2017 recent revisions of Title IX and a reexamination of sexual assault definitions, relied on by colleges, there may be various changes to what constitutes sexual assault between students and between professors and students.[12]

All that has to happen is to change a definition within law, and once-actionable behaviors become tolerable, if not legal. The issue of consent is involved primarily with sex between professors and their students. But things are changing even at colleges and universities. Some of these changes are addressed later in this chapter.[13]

TEACHERS PHYSICALLY ASSAULTING STUDENTS

There has definitely been a shift in the use of social media, prompting an escalation of emotions. Inflammatory remarks being made by teachers toward students are captured and shared with the world online. The age of instant emotion characterized by emojis and emoticons and short videos can produce a heightening of anger and mood shifts. Often, teachers are the subject of what is shared by students, and what is shared is hardly flattering.

In far too many classrooms in America, teachers have to battle with students over their inappropriate use of cell phones during class. These battles sometimes escalate into verbal and physical altercations between teachers and students. Other times, teachers are drawn into precarious situations by attempting to break up fights between students and then becoming involved in the melee.[14] It appears teachers today are being sucked into a vortex of students' outlandish behaviors.

Table 6.1. Five Examples of Teachers Arrested/Convicted of Sexual Assaults of Students

City and State	Name, Title, and School	Date and Offense	Outcome
Shaker Heights, Ohio	Timothy Mitchell IB Diploma Programme Coordinator *Shaker Heights High School*	Early 2000s and 2016 Indicted on charge of sexual battery	Pleaded guilty to child endangerment. Surrendered teaching license.
Hebron, Kentucky	Clinton Bell Teacher *Conner High School*	February–May 2017 Charged with abuse and unlawful use of electronic means to induce a minor to engage in sexual or other prohibited activities	Originally held on $100,000 bond; case pending.
Portland, Maine	Jill Lamontagne Health Teacher *Kennebunk High School*	2017 Indicted on charges of sexual assault of a minor	Booked on charges and released on $1,000 bail. Placed on administrative leave in June 2017. Filed for family medical leave. Resigned from teaching job in September 2017. Arraigned December 2017.
San Juan Capistrano, California	Christian Hernandez Music Teacher *Los Rios Rock School*	2001, 2016 Arrested on suspicion of sexually assaulting a teenage girl	Case remains open and under investigation in 2017.
Milwaukee, Wisconsin	Katherine R. Gonzalez Fifth-Grade Teacher *Atlas Preparatory Academy*	2017 Sexual assault of a child	Sentenced to five years in prison for second-degree sexual assault of a child, plus seven additional years on extended supervision.

What Is Going On?

In 2016, a Modesto, California, third-grade teacher, named Prospero Palmerin, of James Marshall Elementary School was accused of assaulting a *disobedient* student by grabbing him by the shirt. The assault apparently left scratch marks on the student's neck according to the parents. Law enforcement officials recommended that Palmerin be charged with a misdemeanor. However, no charges were filed, and Palmerin was back in the classroom after a paid five-week hiatus.[15]

At East Middle School in Farmington Hills, Michigan, "an 11-year-old student who sat during the Pledge of Allegiance,"[16] was pulled up out of his seat by a female teacher. The parents claimed that this was a violation of the student's civil rights and that when a teacher places his or her hands on a student to force a certain way of thinking, such actions are inappropriate.[17]

In El Paso, Texas, a bilingual teacher with a supposed excellent reputation was arrested a second time for assaulting students. Her second arrest involved "slapping a 5-year-old student."[18] She apparently had been accused in the recent past of several assaults of students. The allegations from previous claims were founded on scant evidence, but the teacher was transferred by her district to another school anyway.

Teachers have been arrested for assaulting students sexually and physically in greater numbers since the 2000s. Some of those arrested were arrested for repeated and numerous acts of sexual assaults upon children.[19] School districts are now beginning to post work chronologies of those accused of assaulting students.[20] The array of charges applied range from sexual assaults and losing control of one's temper and swearing to slapping and hitting students,[21] tying them to chairs,[22] and even taping their mouths to keep them quiet.[23]

These types of assaults are not just found in K–12 *public* schools. Assaults of students are found in every type of school,[24] including at the college level. For example, a California State University, Fullerton part-time professor "allegedly assaulted a College Republicans member in broad daylight during a demonstration against President Trump." The battery was recorded and a report was filed.[25]

In another college example, two former Stanford University English professors had been accused of raping and physically assaulting two graduate students at the University of California, Berkeley, back in the mid-1980s. One of the victims, Kimberly Latta, now a psychotherapist and yoga instructor, was a student of now-deceased Jay Fliegelman. She claims the visiting English instructor "sexually stalked, pressured, and raped,"[26] her while she was attending Berkeley. Fliegelman was eventually "suspended without pay for two years and banned from the department."[27]

One thing that teachers and professors have to guard against is the allegation of wrongdoing for some sort of vendetta or revenge on the part of students and parents. False allegations also know no public and private school distinctions. Likewise, there are no religious denominational schools that are outside the bounds of allegations or potential allegations.[28]

The culture at some of today's institutions of higher learning is captured well by K. A. Amienne. She writes:

> Anytime you have a highly competitive system in which a single person has the power to make or break someone else's career—whether it's the crowded, greasy pole of Hollywood or a flooded Ph.D. pipeline—you will have abuse. Not only rape and overt sexual aggression, but also many complicated and twisted forms of abuse. . . . Institutions need to own up to their systemic mechanisms for abuse and help to solve the problem rather than perpetuate it. We need . . . pedagogical ethics to be a part of every curriculum. We need to educate educators about what abuse is—how to spot it, how to stop it, how to speak up. And we need to give people access to mechanisms for doing so.[29]

TEACHERS VERBALLY ASSAULTING STUDENTS

Although more difficult to prove, verbal assaults of students probably take place more often than physical altercations and sexual assaults. Such abuse, couched in personalized attacks through sarcasm, hurts today's students deeply. All a teacher has to do is to check social media to see the effects of his or her comments to students. Technology is not the friend of the verbally abusive teacher, which is an obvious understatement.

When teachers lose their cool in class, clandestine photos and videos are taken by students. These are quickly shared. They often show students and teachers arguing when tempers flare and tensions escalate. Some students think it is humorous to watch a teacher explode in anger in a classroom. At every moment, teachers must guard how their comments come across to students. Teacher comments or sarcasm directed at today's Gen Z students touch sensitivities toward easy offense. Gen Z does not think twice about using the social media–driven tactic of *group payback*.

The Verbal Abuser

Some teachers are verbally abusive and demeaning to students. For example, Nicholas Frank, an elementary teacher in New Haven, Connecticut, among other things, "was accused of verbally abusing one of his students. . . . Frank pinched his cheeks . . . also ridiculed K's weight calling him derogatory names like 'birthing mother' and 'pregnant.'"[30]

Frank was suspended for eight days for his confirmed treatment of the student. In fact, "Frank's emotional mistreatment of K ultimately landed him on a state central registry for child abuse and neglect."[31] Frank sued asking the Connecticut Supreme Court to settle the question as to whether a classroom teacher could "be placed on a state child abuse registry for verbal barbs aimed at a student during school."[32]

The outcome of the court's decision was most telling, if not foreboding. The court held "It should be obvious to anyone, let alone a professional educator, that this type of behavior—the targeting of a particular student's physical characteristics in a demeaning and hurtful way—would fall within the terms 'degrading' or 'victimizing' . . . and therefore enough to qualify for the child abuse registry."[33]

Targeting

Verbal bantering and throwing barbs can today be considered targeting. Such is the case with a recent incident involving a teacher from Georgia's Rockdale Career Academy in Conyers. Paul Hagan "got angry because a group of students kept laughing in class"[34] and not paying attention. The teacher was recorded as saying, "I'm serious dude. If you screw with me, you're going to get in big trouble. . . . Don't smile at me, man. That's how people like you get shot. I got a bet by the time you're 21 somebody's gonna put a bullet right through your head. Okay? And it might be me the one who does it."[35] Hagan was placed on administrative leave.

Even teacher–student jovial jousting has to be tempered by making certain specific lines are not crossed and that students do not feel hurt by the bantering back and forth. Students are the center of the education universe, and their emotions are their primary mode of interpreting reality. What one person means by fun, another may take as harmful. That being said, however, the teacher is always held to a higher standard. This is especially an issue for more veteran teachers from previous generations when certain words and teasing seemed to have been allowed under a different set of cultural norms. The same words used years ago if used today may result in legal action.

Protected class status and a more litigious culture are new cultural norms. Ironically, if a teacher quotes a historical statement in class, he or she runs the risk of escalating emotions. Trigger warnings are often part of the teacher's *get ready for something offensive* disclaimer. If students are offended, the response can be highly retaliatory. Labeling teachers is meant to shame them, and this is a new cultural norm. Certainly, no teacher wants the label of bully or child abuser, particularly by someone easily offended.[36]

VIOLENT TEACHERS IN THE CLASSROOMS

Teachers demonstrating violent behaviors have no place in the classroom. The right to an education does not come with the right for an educator to harm or injure others in the process. Americans would call it shameful if schools had to adjust school culture to a new culture of violence as a norm and just *go with the flow*. Unfortunately, what happens in the larger cultural context in America always flows into our nations' public schools. There is no doubt that we live in a culture that accepts more violence.

Extreme Teacher Behaviors

While many teachers can "understand" why a colleague's frustrations might rise to the level of restraining a student in a chair or taping his mouth shut, it is never all right under the law to resort to these actions. Again, teachers who react with extreme behaviors toward disruptive students have no business in the classroom or working in education at all. Their actions are reactive and abusive and not proactive and self-controlled.

In Public School 194, in Harlem, New York, a convicted public school teacher is "still receiving his six-figure salary . . . even after having attacked a 7-year-old special-needs boy." After classroom disruptions deemed serious enough for the student to be removed from the class, the teacher in question apparently shoved the student "after the boy tried to reenter" the classroom against the teacher's will.

The teacher was sentenced to thirty days in jail for what had been deemed "a completely unjustifiable use of force." The teacher was also on the receiving end of a complaint that he threw a student down a flight of stairs at the school.[37] As a result of these incidents, Osman Couey was reassigned within the New York City Department of Education, away from students, and retains his $105,142 annual salary.

While it is true that unless a person actually experiences daily behaviors of students who simply will not comply, there is little understanding of the emotional and physical drain. It is also true that some teachers should not remain in the profession, protected by unions that make it nearly impossible to get rid of poor teachers.[38]

We live at a time when it seems the iconoclasts and the unruly seem to be gaining traction in American culture. For example, in some cities people can assault police and be hailed as heroes, whereas these same police using retaliatory force to restore order are somehow crossing the line. Those on the receiving end of the police actions claim they are victims of hate and excessive force, even when the police have not acted as aggressors.

In many places, police are constrained from intervening because of the threats of lawsuits against the them. In some ways, teachers are similar to police. Citizens expect both to take the abuse and do very little about it in return. Similarly, students in schools can destroy property and bully and assault classmates and their teachers, yet when disciplined, these students and their families claim the teacher is the guilty party.

Teachers hitting students or involving themselves in fistfights is a new low in education. Maybe it is time to revisit laws and reemphasize the role of the teacher as a respectful authority figure and the balance of what this means within the context of a twenty-first-century America. The promotion and tolerance of factional partisanship breeds its own kind, usually with terse words and coarse behaviors associated with them. Could it be that American education is too far down the road to return to decency because American culture has tanked?

Teachers and students are not equals, and certainly, students are not the center of the universe, much to their chagrin. Is it too late for our schools to reverse certain trends and do what is both appropriate and advantageous for all? The nation's public schools may be too accommodating to be successful. If either of these turns out to be true, public education may be on its last legs.

EXTREME MEASURES: TAPED MOUTHS AND CUFFED HANDS

Undoubtedly, the general public has come across stories on the Internet or from their local news that report that some teachers duct-taped the mouths of their students to keep them quiet. For some time now, people have probably read about autistic students who had to be restrained in classrooms as a result of their behaviors causing harm to others.

While such actions on the parts of teachers sound abusive and ridiculous, one can be certain that the thoughts of such restraints have crossed the minds of more and more teachers while on the job. Keeping students seated and focused to accomplish even the most basic of educational expectations is sometimes mission impossible for some teachers.

No one advocates extreme measures with students unless there are actions warranted to meet the extremes. For example, removing a student from an elementary class while the student is screaming and throwing things across the room in the process is probably a good thing. Physically restraining a student from self-injury and possibly injuring others is also a good thing but now comes at a cost. The cost may be the teacher's job.

Teachers must be trained on proper holds and proper amounts of pressure to restrain. These holds are subject to criticism, and the teacher can be accountable for marks left on a violent child. In other words, people actually have to be trained in the legal ways to hold a child to avoid being sued. This is why many teachers no longer break up fights on their campuses.

Proactive Instead of Reactive?

Personal anecdotes can be quite convincing in terms of making a point in dealing with students expressing violent actions. Teachers sharing their stories give a corporate voice that is often muzzled by schools and their districts.

As teachers, there is no longer assurance that violent students can be restrained in time to avoid injuring themselves and others.

Some teachers are beginning to think twice about their passivity toward being injured or whether they should lay their hands on students in defending themselves, even at the prospect of losing their jobs. Some choose safety over job. Obviously, the older the student attacker, the more physical defense becomes an issue. But this does raise a dilemma for the assaulted teacher.

In terms of younger students, defending against being injured is vastly different than meeting force with force upon violent assaults brought about by older and much larger students. A recent case in Antioch, California, is evidence that a teacher was not going to allow a student to beat on her. So she fought back with a thirteen-year-old after she had been hit several times in the face and knocked to the ground by the assailant. [39]

Deflecting an assault before it occurs by disarming a student's rage is one good method to deter violence. But a teacher has to know students well enough to be able to de-escalate situations before assaults occur. Certainly, if a student takes things too far and strikes a teacher or is throwing objects or making what appears to be threatening moves in his or her direction, then a teacher has the right to neutralize the situation. In fact, the teacher has the right to immobilize the student, if that is possible.

Having another student run for help is another option. Schools should have advanced technology available for teachers to wear with a school lanyard that when pressed sends an immediate emergency signal to school security, 911, or both. Students will know this technology exists, and there is the possibility that its existence could act as a deterrent to violence in some cases. Any actions taken by teachers that repel students' assaults will be examined with the highest levels of scrutiny.

GUNS ON CAMPUSES?

Some states are allowing teachers to carry guns onto campuses as protection against active shooters. To date, there have been no public reports of teachers threatening students with their guns or students getting ahold of these guns.

Some states' legislators have mixed emotions at what to do about arming certain staff members on public school campuses. [40] This brings up another valid concern. If teachers are armed and carry weapons on campus, angry students or those with violent tendencies might somehow gain access to one of the on-campus weapons. At that time, the purpose of self-defense would have been turned on its head. A very real scenario would play out should a second teacher have to take down a student who commandeered the first teacher's weapon.

As an educator, it is difficult even to envision a time when the need to pull a gun on a student might arise. It seems beyond the rational to threaten the use of a gun in class to regain control during an assault. However, we live during irrational times, and some imbalanced adults are placed inside classrooms to teach students.

With the Columbine High School and Sandy Hook Elementary School massacres and other school shootings still ingrained in the national psyche, seeking such options is certainly understandable and within contextual reactions. Although these reactions are understandable, they remain the most unconscionable of last resort as a means to end students' assaults of teachers. [41]

The most obvious question in any discussion regarding teachers with concealed guns is what happens if a student overpowers a teacher with a gun and uses it on the teacher and the students? Education associations have weighed in on this matter with mixed feelings and different frames of mind.

> An NEA poll of 800 members in January 2013 found that educators opposed arming school employees. Only 22% of NEA members polled favored firearms training for teachers and other school employees and letting them carry firearms in schools; 61% strongly opposed the proposal. Members of the Association of American Educators, the country's largest national, non-union professional teacher association, expressed mixed feelings on safety and gun issues. The results of a poll conducted in February found 61% of those responding supported a proposed Arkansas policy that would allow educators access to a locked, concealed firearm after a training course. [42]

Recent Legislation

In mid-October 2017, the governor of California signed a bill removing the authority of district administrators to grant permission for teachers to bring concealed weapons onto campus. "State law already prohibited civilians who are not school workers from bringing firearms onto school grounds, but a change in the law last year gave school district superintendents power to decide whether they would let their employees carry." [43]

Approximately eighteen other states already allow concealed firearms, with few restrictions. One of the arguments is that they could have prevented the massacres at schools from occurring had one or more teachers been armed. [44] Currently, "all 50 states allow citizens to carry concealed weapons if they meet certain state requirements." [45]

There is also the possibility of fifty-state reciprocity of concealed carry weapons on the part of handgun owners. However, both of these instances would probably not apply to arming teachers on school campuses. However, the ultimate decisions will be left up to the states, and "currently, there are 16 states that ban carrying a concealed weapon on a college campus: Califor-

nia, Florida, Illinois, Louisiana, Massachusetts, Michigan, Missouri, Nebraska, Nevada, New Jersey, New Mexico, New York, North Carolina, North
Dakota, South Carolina and Wyoming."[46]

THE CONTINUING PROBLEMS OF INAPPROPRIATE TEACHER–STUDENT RELATIONSHIPS

Inappropriate relationships with students occur when certain boundaries are
crossed by teachers and others in positions of educational authority.[47] With
respect to teachers, they should not be expected to be all things to all students
professionally or personally. Boundaries of relational proximity should be
respected at all time between teachers and students. Educators should never
be expected to cross over from professional into personal relationships with
students.[48] As anyone who works with students knows, "The system thrusts
humans with raging hormones closely together in work environments. Competitions and 'play' conditions force proximities and are sometimes abrasive
to moral boundaries."[49]

States have reported increases in arrests of teachers having illegal relationships with their students, beginning in elementary school. This is true for
both male and female teachers.[50] Assaults and predation are found without
regard for age, gender, or sexual orientation.

Education professionals must question why these relationships develop as
well as the reasons teachers are willing to risk their families, careers, and
freedom to engage in criminal, sexual relationships with their students. Interestingly, more women than men seem to be making headlines for arrests
these days. Where are the intervention programs and professional development for teacher candidates and veteran teachers already on the job? Guidelines and professional development are needed today.

PREDATION PROBLEMS

Schools and colleges of education are stepping up efforts to incorporate
training regarding boundaries that exist between generations.[51] However,
because of teacher attrition, there is often a rush to press student teachers or
interns into action. Who can resist being given the opportunity to grow into
the education profession, earn a paycheck, and achieve significant professional experiences without necessarily having all the prerequisites accomplished in preparation for the positions?[52]

This is especially problematic for younger and newer teachers and
coaches. These classroom novices are expected to teach students who are
sometimes quite close to them in age. To the point, there has been a rise in
predation among young teachers and their students.[53] This is very alarming,

but what makes it even more alarming is that there is not just one profile of a sexual predator.

Predators are smart and savvy in their uses of social media[54] and often use it to their advantage. This is problematic for children and teenagers since their developing brains are highly vulnerable to social and emotional engagement by predator types.[55] Teachers should not hang out online with students.

SEXUAL RELATIONSHIPS BETWEEN COLLEGE FACULTY AND STUDENTS

There is no secret that college campuses have had a terrible time cutting down on sexual assaults on their campuses. Again and again, campus administrators revisit their policies of faculty and student relationships, as sexual assaults and sexual harassment have become lightning rod issues on college campuses.[56]

At far too many universities, although frowned upon, there is no policy preventing professors and students from engaging in intimate or sexual relationships. There is a general understanding that underclassmen are less likely to be approached by faculty than are graduate students. However, this is not always the case, and there are obstacles to drawing the boundaries.

Rather than external policing of professors and their relationships with students, faculty unions opt rather for what can be called internal policing rather than an outright ban of romantic and sexual relationships. For example:

> Northwestern University mirrors a typical, contemporary university policy regarding faculty and student romantic and sexual relationships, as it pertains to professors and undergraduates, professors and graduate students, and coaches and players. In terms of the professor-undergraduate relationship, there is complete prohibition. "Consensual romantic or sexual relationships between faculty and students or coaches and students, even absent any supervisory or evaluative authority, may lead to unanticipated conflicts of interest since a teacher's or coach's influence and power may extend beyond the classroom, department, or team. There is always the possibility that the faculty member or coach may unexpectedly be placed in a position of power over the student."[57]

Specifically, as a result of the disparity in power between undergraduates and faculty and/or coaches, the inherent risks are greater if romantic or sexual relationships develop. To illustrate the point:

> Due to the institutional power differential in faculty-student and coach-student relationships, there is the inherent risk of coercion and the perception by others of exploitation. When undergraduate students are involved, the difference in institutional power and the inherent risk of coercion are so great that *no faculty*

member or coaching staff member shall enter into a romantic, dating, or sexual relationship with a Northwestern undergraduate student, regardless of whether there is a supervisory or evaluative relationship between them.[58]

The relationships between professors and graduate and professional students are less restricted, but when a professor has a supervisory role over the student, there is a shift in the policy. Accordingly, Northwestern's policy states: "Romantic or sexual relationships between faculty and graduate/professional students are also problematic. *No faculty member shall enter into a romantic, dating, or sexual relationship with a Northwestern graduate/professional student under his/her supervision.* Should such a relationship begin, the department chair must be notified promptly so that arrangements for alternative supervision and removal of evaluative authority can be made."[59]

In 2015, Harvard University updated its policy. Now, it has "banned its faculty members from having sex with undergraduates, revising a conduct policy that school officials decided did not sufficiently recognize the 'unequal status' between professors and students. The new policy amends a conduct policy to say that 'no . . . faculty member shall request or accept sexual favors from, or initiate or engage in a romantic or sexual relationship with, any undergraduate student at Harvard College' . . . also . . . professors may not have sexual relations with graduate students who are under their 'academic supervision.'"[60]

Other universities, such as Yale, and a small group of others have followed Harvard's lead. Restricting sexual relationships due to conflicts of interest and the possibility of misuse of power and influence to gain sexual favors are main drivers of new, more restrictive policies. Another main consideration is sexual assault and sexual harassment policies.

Circumstances have forced colleges, under Title IX, to reexamine their long-standing polices about sexual assault, sexual harassment, and consensual romantic or sexual relationships between faculty and students.[61] Resistance to these restrictions has been strong from the American Association of University Professors (AAUP), opting instead for professors to be wise and to understand their choices have consequences and questioned where to draw the lines between "protecting people from unequal relationships and unnecessarily interfering in people's personal lives."[62]

The AAUP was not particularly pleased that faculty and student relationships were banned in many instances. Likewise, some student groups also complained that some of their autonomy as adults was being stripped away. They claimed, "We're grownups . . . we can choose with whom we have sex."[63] The problems persist from K–16 and beyond into graduate school. Education policy experts as practitioners had better decide to act sooner rather than later.

WHAT NEEDS TO BE DONE

Professional development today should be more practical and relevant. Districts focus on the curricular aspects necessary for academic achievement in schools. However, the issues that are left out of professional development are often what are needed to accomplish the academics in the first place.

Pressures facing teachers are very different today than just a few years ago. Professional development has to change to reflect these differences. Teachers are assaulting students, and they need to be made aware of ways to control themselves and the situations in which they find themselves about to be compromised. There will always be sessions for teachers on presenting new curriculum, assessments, and so on. But where are the tools for teachers handling the stresses associated with students who provoke and display violent behaviors?

The least that school districts can do is to require students with violent tendencies to be placed in classes, as well as make it more difficult to suspend, to provide training on keeping one's temper under control. Teachers are fed up, and they are either hitting back or lashing out first by assaulting students. This needs to change. Schools are not protecting teachers, and they are not training them to handle what Gen Z students are throwing their way.

Rather than planning curriculum and discussions of pacing calendars, professional development should focus on strategies to protect oneself and ways to neutralize students without causing either side any injury. Unlike in the past, there exists today the necessity of addressing proactivity in areas of educator actions in classrooms as well as appropriate teacher–student relationships.

Boundaries are good things for K–12 teachers and students. Boundaries are good things for college professors and college students as well. Moreover, moral and legal boundaries are equally as good for teachers, professors, and anyone who works with students at any level. Professional development must call into question these boundaries, their establishment, and their application and consequences when they are violated. Teachers need to know what will happen when they hit a student for any reason, including self-defense.

Educators who know how to set and reinforce boundaries are intuitively focusing on higher levels of professionalism and respect. Schools need more of this from teachers. Thus, the best approach for an educator is never to enter an emotional, physical, or sexual relationship with a student for any reason, minor or otherwise.

Colleges and universities are right in moving toward banning sexual relationships between professors and students. The time has come to establish such boundaries. The education profession must become more diligent in restricting relationships that cross these lines. Sex and compromise between professors and students are often twin motivators. The outcomes of these motivators as actions bring with them unintended consequences.

At a time when sexual assault accusations are running rampant, professional development is needed more than ever. For today's educators, relationship mistakes with students not only violate policy but may now be illegal in their states. Aside from ruining families, affecting the psychological and emotional makeup of the young and impressionable, such assaults with minors can be career stoppers and ruin relationships for the victims when they grow into adulthood.

As with all other abuse and assaults, sexual assaults should never be found in America's schools, among America's students, and certainly not among our nation's teachers. The time for change is now.

NOTES

1. Grace Lougheed and Julia Barragate. "Mitchell's victim speaks." *The Shakerite*. October 13, 2017. Retrieved from https://shakerite.com/top-stories/2017/10/13/mitchells-victim-speaks/.

2. Caroline Glenn. "Palm Bay teacher fired for biting special needs student." *Florida Today*. March 14, 2017. Retrieved from www.floridatoday.com/story/news/2017/03/14/palm-bay-teacher-fired-biting-special-needs-student/99148806/.

3. Tim Walker. "Hiring non-certified teachers no way to address teacher shortage, say experts." *NEA Today*. March 23, 2016. Retrieved from http://neatoday.org/2016/03/23/teacher-shortage-non-certified-teachers/.

4. Stephanie Zacharek, Eliana Dockterman, and Haley Sweetland Edwards. "The silence breakers." *Time*. December 18, 2017. Retrieved from http://time.com/time-person-of-the-year-2017-silence-breakers/.

5. Jason Kotowski. "Rise in sex crimes in schools coincides with proliferation of social media, attorney says." July 2, 2017. *The Bakersfield Californian*, pp. A1, A5.

6. Doug Criss. "The (incomplete) list of powerful men accused of sexual harassment after Harvey Weinstein." *CNN*. November 1, 2017. Retrieved from www.cnn.com/2017/10/25/us/list-of-accused-after-weinstein-scandal-trnd/index.html.

7. James Vaznis. "Mass. sees increase in educator misconduct investigations." *The Boston Globe*. October 19, 2017. Retrieved from www.bostonglobe.com/metro/2017/10/19/mass-sees-increase-educator-misconduct-investigations/Y63Zd77ynGFTTdk75PpnkM/amp.html.

8. Joy Resmovits. "Marlborough school settles suit by former student who was sexually abused by teacher." *Los Angeles Times*. October 4, 2015. Retrieved from www.latimes.com/local/education/la-me-marlborough-settlement-20171004-story.html.

9. Ernest J. Zarra III. *Teacher-student relationships: Crossing into the emotional, physical, and sexual realms*. 2013. Lanham, MD: Rowman & Littlefield.

10. Everton Bailey. "Substitute teacher who abused students had faced repeated reprimands in Portland." *Oregon City News*. October 24, 2017. Retrieved from www.oregonlive.com/oregon-city/index.ssf/2017/10/substitute_teacher_who_abused.html.

11. Minyvonne Burke. "Substitute teacher at Christian school accused of kissing student." *New York Daily News*. November 1, 2017. Retrieved from www.nydailynews.com/news/crime/substitute-teacher-christian-school-accused-kissing-student-article-1.3604421?cid=aol. Cf. Staff. "Substitute teacher, 23, physically removed from class over sex allegations with teen students." *FOX NEWS*. November 9, 2017. Retrieved from www.foxnews.com/us/2017/11/09/substitute-teacher-23-physically-removed-from-class-over-sex-allegations-with-teen-students.html.

12. Staff. "DeVos' change to Title IX guidance on sex assault investigations prompts suit." *NBC News*. October 20, 2017. Retrieved from www.nbcnews.com/news/us-news/devos-change-title-ix-guidance-sex-assault-investigations-prompts-suit-n812521. Cf. Mara Rose Williams. "Former student alleges KU didn't investigate claims a professor sexually assaulted him." *The Kansas City Star*. April 5, 2017. Retrieved from www.kansascity.com/news/local/article142823104.html. Cf. also, Whitney Bermes. "Former student claims she was raped by music professor, sues MSU." *Bozeman Daily Chronicle*. October 17, 2013. Retrieved from www.bozemandailychronicle.com/news/montana_state_university/former-student-claims-she-was-raped-by-music-professor-sues/article_d94aaa9a-376b-11e3-b0fa-001a4bcf887a.html.

13. Lougheed and Barragate. "Mitchell's victim speaks." Cf. the following. Staff. "Northern Kentucky teacher accused of inappropriate contact with student." *WLWT5*. October 13, 2017. Retrieved from www.wlwt.com/article/northern-kentucky-teacher-accused-of-inappropriate-contact-with-student/12919748; Staff. "Married Maine teacher indicted for multiple sex romps with student who tried to commit suicide." *FOX NEWS*. October 4, 2017. Retrieved from www.foxnews.com/us/2017/10/04/married-maine-teacher-indicted-on-14-sexual-assault-charges-with-student-who-tried-to-commit-suicide.html; Staff. "Authorities search for more possible victims of former teacher accused of sexually assaulting student." *NBC Los Angeles*. August 25, 2017. Retrieved from www.nbclosangeles.com/news/local/San-Juan-Capistrano-music-teacher-sex-assault-441768923.html; Staff. "Female teacher, 25, gets prison for 'sexual contact' with boy while watching 'Deadpool.'" *FOX NEWS*. September 29, 2017. Retrieved from www.foxnews.com/us/2017/09/29/female-teacher-25-had-sex-romp-with-boy-student-11-while-watching-deadpool.html.

14. Editors. "Video of Georgia teacher caught up in student fight shocks community." *Fox News*. September 22, 2017. Retrieved from www.foxnews.com/us/2017/09/22/video-georgia-teacher-caught-up-in-student-fight-shocks-community.html.

15. Nan Austin. "Parents say Modesto teacher attacked their son." *The Modesto Bee*. August 15, 2016. Retrieved from www.modbee.com/news/local/education/article95874442.html.

16. Carla Herreria. "Teacher accused of assaulting student for sitting during pledge of allegiance." *Huffington Post*. September 16, 2017. Retrieved from www.huffingtonpost.com/entry/michigan-teacher-assaults-student-pledge-of-allegiance_us_59bd9a27e4b0edff971c99e2.

17. Herreria. "Teacher accused of assaulting student."

18. Staff. "Kindergarten teacher arrested again for assaulting student." *New York Post*. October 3, 2017. Retrieved from http://nypost.com/2017/10/03/kindergarten-teacher-arrested-again-for-assaulting-student/.

19. Bill Novak. "Madison elementary school teacher arrested, allegedly sexually assaulted student, police say." *Wisconsin State Journal*. October 13, 2017. Retrieved from http://host.madison.com/wsj/news/local/crime/madison-elementary-school-teacher-arrested-allegedly-sexually-assaulted-student-police/article_8038101c-5ecd-5679-aaa2-b3c8f1434eba.html.

20. Michael Konopasek and Staff. "Middle school teacher suspected of sexually assaulting students." *FOX 31*. August 22, 2017. Retrieved from http://kdvr.com/2017/08/22/police-cherry-creek-teacher-suspect-in-sexual-assault-case-that-may-involve-multiple-victims/.

21. Kimberly Eiten. "PTO meets with school after teacher charged with assaulting student." *CBS Baltimore*. May 10, 2017. Retrieved from http://baltimore.cbslocal.com/2017/05/10/teacher-assault-meeting/.

22. Sara Gates. "Fresno teacher allegedly tied student to chair because he wouldn't remain seated (video)." *Huffington Post*. February 1, 2013. Retrieved from www.huffingtonpost.com/2013/02/01/teacher-tied-unruly-student-chair-bakman-elementary_n_2598882.html.

23. Jessica Schladebeck. "Teacher duct tapes students' mouths at Texas elementary school." *New York Daily News*. October 20, 2017. Retrieved from www.nydailynews.com/news/national/teacher-duct-tapes-students-mouths-texas-elementary-school-article-1.3576588. Cf. Kristine Phillips. "She won't be quiet!!!!: Teacher accused of taping the mouth of a student with cerebral palsy." *The Washington Post*. November 5, 2017. Retrieved from www.washingtonpost.com/news/education/wp/2017/11/05/she-wont-be-quiet-teacher-accused-of-taping-the-mouth-of-a-student-with-cerebral-palsy/?utm_term=.f93c0c862a2c.

24. Cristina Maze. "Christian teacher accused of raping students for years, charged with 84 counts of sexual abuse." *Newsweek*. November 10, 2017. Retrieved from www.newsweek.com/christian-teacher-rape-sex-abuse-school-students-708377.

25. Peter Van Voorhis. "CSUF prof allegedly assaults conservative student on campus." *Campus Reform*. February 9, 2017. Retrieved from www.campusreform.org/?ID=8763. Cf. Harry Shukman. "My professor has just been charged with assaulting me." *The Tab*. September 25, 2017. Retrieved from https://thetab.com/us/2017/09/25/judy-morelock-charged-for-assault-72044. Cf. also George Kelly and Rick Hurd. "Bay area college professor used U-shaped bike lock in beating, police say." *East Bay Times*. June 1, 2017. Retrieved from https://www.eastbaytimes.com/2017/05/24/berkeley-college-professor-arrested-as-assault-suspect/.

26. Katherine Mangan. "2 women say Stanford Professors raped them years ago." *The Chronicle of Higher Education*. November 11, 2017. Retrieved from www.chronicle.com/article/2-Women-Say-Stanford/241749?cid=wcontentlist_hp_latest.

27. Mangan. "2 women say Stanford Professors raped them years ago."

28. Scott Orr. "When a teacher is falsely accused, what happens?" *The Daily Courier*. March 7, 2017. Retrieved from www.dcourier.com/news/2017/mar/07/when-teacher-falsely-accused-what-happens/.

29. K. A. Amienne. "Abusers and enablers in faculty culture." *The Chronicle of Higher Education*. November 2, 2017. Retrieved from www.chronicle.com/article/AbusersEnablers-in/241648?cid=wcontentgrid_hp_2.

30. Staff. "Ed law briefly: Teacher who verbally insults young student can be listed on a statewide child abuse registry." *Real Clear Education*. September 16, 2014. Retrieved from www.realcleareducation.com/articles/2014/09/16/ed_law_briefly_teacher_who_verbally_insults_young_student__can_be_listed_on_a_statewide_child_abuse_registry_1103.html.

31. Ibid.

32. Ibid.

33. Ibid.

34. Minyvonne Burke. "See it: Teacher placed on leave after he threatens to 'put a bullet' in student's head." *New York Daily News*. November 8, 2017. Retrieved from www.aol.com/article/news/2017/11/08/see-it-teacher-placed-on-leave-after-he-threatens-to-put-a-bullet-in-students-head/23270698/.

35. Ibid.

36. Tina Burnside. "Cops: Teacher told girl to kill herself, forced other kids to bully her." *CNN*. April 28, 2017. Retrieved from www.cnn.com/2017/04/28/us/teachers-bullied-girl-trnd/index.html.

37. Justin Haskins. "Teacher attacked 7-year-old special-needs boy—but what happened next might be even more outrageous." *The Blaze*. April 23, 2017. Retrieved from www.theblaze.com/news/2017/04/23/teacher-attacked-7-year-old-special-needs-boy-but-what-happened-next-might-be-even-more-outrageous/.

38. Ibid.

39. Rowena Coetsee. "Antioch: 13-year-old girl cited for beating middle-school teacher." *Mercury News*. February 4, 2017. Retrieved from www.mercurynews.com/2017/02/02/antioch-punishing-students-for-big-offenses-can-be-complicated/.

40. Staff. "Guns on campus: Overview." *National Conference of State Legislatures*. May 5, 2017. Retrieved from www.ncsl.org/research/education/guns-on-campus-overview.aspx.

41. Kate Murphy. "New laws: Teachers do not have to disclose guns." *USA Today*. August 19, 2014. Retrieved from www.usatoday.com/story/news/nation/2014/08/19/teachers-guns-schools-news21/14103875/.

42. Ibid.

43. Staff. "Gov. Brown signs new bill banning all guns on school campuses." *ABC 30 News*. October 14, 2017. Retrieved from http://abc30.com/politics/gov-brown-signs-new-bill-banning-all-guns-on-school-campuses/2534055/.

44. Staff. "Guns in schools: Firearms already allowed in 18 states with few restrictions." *Huffington Post*. January 15, 2013. Retrieved from www.huffingtonpost.com/2013/01/15/guns-in-schools-firearms-_n_2482168.html.

45. Ibid.

46. Ibid.

47. Zarra, *Teacher-student relationships*, p. 18.

48. Ed Richter. "Female gym teacher accused of sex acts with football players." *Dayton Daily News*. February 8, 2011. Retrieved from www.daytondailynews.com/news/crime--law/female-gym-teacher-accused-sex-acts-with-football-players/h9lGubinZ9WeQxjj1tWvYK/. Cf. Barbara Walters. "Mary K. Letourneau: Biography." *Biography*. April 20, 2015. Retrieved from www.biography.com/people/mary-kay-letourneau-9542379.

49. Zarra, *Teacher-student relationships*, p. 18.

50. Amy Oliver. *Sex education: Why are so many female teachers having affairs with their teenage students . . . and is the cougar effect to blame?* May 28, 2011. Retrieved from www.dailymail.co.uk/news/article-1391626/Whats-wrong-female-teachers-America-As-schools-summer-young-teacher-arrested-sex-16-year-old-student--latestdozens-cases-school-year.html.

51. Zarra, *Teacher-student relationships*, pp. 18ff.

52. Linda Darling-Hammond. "The challenge of staffing our schools." *Educational Leadership*, 2001. Vol. 58, No. 8, pp. 12–17. Cf. Heather Voke. *Understanding and responding to the teacher shortage* . 2002. Washington, DC: Association for Supervision and Curriculum Development.

53. Janis Wolak, David Finkelhor, Michelle L. Ybarra, et al. "Online 'predators' and their victims: Myths, realities, and implications for prevention and treatment." February–March 2008. *American Psychologist*. Vol. 63, No. 2, pp. 111–128.

54. Craig Hlavaty. "Students, teachers and social media get a second look in light of recent criminal incidents." *The Houston Chronicle*. June 15, 2016. Retrieved from www.chron.com/news/houstontexas/houston/article/Students-teachers-and-social-media-8106030.php. Cf. Abbie Alford. "Social media fueling teacher and student relationships." *Fox News.* May 23, 2012. Retrieved from http://www.fox23.com/news/breaking-news/social-media-fueling-teacher-student-sexual-relati/254263587.

55. Harry Barry and Edna Murphy. *Flagging the screenager: Guiding your child through adolescence and young adulthood*. 2014. Dublin, Ireland: Liberties Press, pp. 37–55.

56. Rebecca Schuman. "Hands off your grad students!" *Slate*. July 6, 2014. Retrieved from www.slate.com/articles/life/education/2014/07/professors_and_advisers_having_sexual_relationships_with_grad_students_hurts.html.

57. Office of the Provost. "Consensual romantic or sexual relationships between faculty, staff, and students." *Northwestern University*. January 13, 2014. Retrieved from http://policies.northwestern.edu/docs/Consensual_Relations_011314.pdf. Cf. Office of the Provost. "Newly added policies: Sexual misconduct." *Northwestern University*. September 5, 2017. Retrieved from http://policies.northwestern.edu/newly-added/index.html.

58. Ibid.

59. Ibid.

60. Editors. "Harvard University bans sex between professors and undergraduate students." *NBC News*. February 6, 2015. Retrieved from www.nbcnews.com/news/education/harvard-university-bans-sex-between-professors-undergraduate-students-n301451.

61. Susan Svrluga. "Harvard formally bans sexual relationships between professors and undergrads." *The Washington Post*. February 5, 2015. Retrieved from https://www.washingtonpost.com/news/grade-point/wp/2015/02/05/harvard-formally-bans-sexual-relationships-between-professors-and-undergrads/?utm_term=.f6c48e0f21ad. Cf. John Lauerman. "Harvard tells profs not to sleep with undergrads." *Bloomberg*. February 5, 2015. Retrieved from www.bloomberg.com/news/articles/2015-02-05/harvard-bans-professors-from-having-sex-with-undergraduates.

62. Ibid.

63. Ibid.

Appendix

Survey of Assaults against Teachers

GENERAL BACKGROUND

1. How many years have you been teaching or in the education profession?
   1–5 (N = 87): 20%
   6–10 (N = 87): 20%
   11–20 (N = 156): 36%
   21 or more (N = 105): 24%
2. What is your age category?
   21–25 (N = 12): 3%
   26–30 (N = 69): 16%
   31–35 (N = 57): 13%
   36–40 (N = 63): 14%
   41–50 (N = 129): 30%
   51–60 (N = 72): 16%
   Older than 61 (N = 33): 8%
3. What is your gender?
   Male (N = 84): 19%
   Female (N = 351): 81%
   Other (N = 0): 0%
4. What is your title? Choose the title that BEST describes your daily work in education.
   Classroom Teacher (N = 310): 71%
   School Site Administrator (ex: Principal/VP) (N = 9): 2%
   School Counselor (N = 6): 2%
   School Psychologist (N = 6): 1%

Educational Specialist (N = 24): 6%

Special Education Teacher (N = 36): 8%

Coach (N = 0): 0%

College Professor (N = 12): 3%

Adjunct College Instructor (N = 6): 1%

Other* (N = 27): 6%

*Other includes write-ins, such as Para-Professional, Assistant Director of Special Education, Speech-Language Pathologist, Education Consultant, Substitute Teacher, School Social Worker, and Minister of Christian Education.

5. In which state or U.S. territory are you employed in education?

The following table of respondents includes only state data and the number of respondents from these states who are employed in education. Note: Washington, DC, was not included as an option in this survey.

6. In which type of educational institution are you employed?

Public School: (N = 366): 84%

Private School: (N = 30): 7%

Charter School: (N = 12): 3%

College or University: (N = 18): 4%

Other* (please specify): (N = 9): 2%

*Other includes write-ins, such as Private Educational Clinic, Court School, and Church.

7. What grade level, class, or oversight assignment is your focus in education?

Administrative (Public School) (N = 6): 1%

Primary (K–3) (N = 117): 27%

Intermediate (4–6) (N = 72): 17%

Junior High/Middle (6–9) (N = 57): 13%

Secondary/High School (9–12) (N = 123): 28%

Administrative (College or University) (N = 0): 0%

College or University (Years 1–4) (N = 18): 4%

College or University (Graduate) (N = 0): 0%

College or University (Post-Graduate) (N = 0): 0%

Other* (please specify) (N = 42): 10%

*Other includes write-ins, such as Diagnostic Assessment Clinician, Special Education (K–12), English for Speakers of Other Languages (ESOL), and various classroom combinations of K–12.

8. Do you work exclusively with special education students?

Yes (N = 48): 11%

No (N = 387): 89%

9. Do you have "special needs" students in your classroom? ("Special needs" is a designation that may include autism spectrum, emotionally disturbed, and oppositional defiance disorders, among others.)

State	Number	State	Number
AL	6	MT	0
AK	3	NE	4
AZ	11	NV	6
AR	8	NH	0
CA	170	NJ	21
CO	6	NM	3
CT	7	NY	22
DE	2	NC	6
FL	20	ND	0
GA	9	OH	6
HI	0	OK	2
ID	0	OR	1
IL	6	PA	9
IN	2	RI	0
IA	3	SC	6
KS	2	SD	0
KY	1	TN	10
LA	0	TX	14
ME	0	UT	10
MD	6	VT	0
MA	7	VA	6
MI	3	WA	18
MN	5	WV	3
MS	3	WI	6
MO	0	WY	2

Yes (N = 393): 90%

No (N = 36): 8%

Other* (please specify) (N = 6): 2%

*Other includes write-ins, such as "I don't have my own classroom" and "I am not certain if my students are special needs."

ASSAULT: GENERAL

10. In your opinion, have you ever been "intentionally" assaulted while working in education?

Yes, definitely (N = 192): 44%
No, never (N = 168): 40%
I think so, but not certain (N = 45): 10%
I do not think so, but not certain (N = 27): 6%
Other (please specify) (N = 3): 0%

11. How many times in the past 1–3 years would you consider an assault of any type to have taken place against you while at work?

None (N = 216): 50%
1–2 times (N = 114): 26%
3–4 times (N = 27): 6%
5–6 times (N = 30): 7%
More than 6 times (N = 30): 7%
It occurs almost on a weekly basis (N = 18): 4%
Other (please specify) (N = 0): 0%

12. If you were assaulted while at work, were your superiors informed about the incident(s)?

Yes (N = 249): 57%
No (N = 15): 4%
Does Not Apply (N = 171): 39%

13. If your superiors were informed of any assault against you, was there a police report filed?

Yes (N = 21): 5%
No (N = 222): 51%
Does Not Apply (N = 192): 44%

14. Have you ever had to receive medical care from an assault that took place at work?

Yes (N = 60): 14%
No (N = 210): 48%
Does Not Apply (N = 165): 38%

15. If you were assaulted while at work, were you satisfied at how the incident(s) was/were handled?

Yes (N = 105): 24%
No (N = 150): 35%
Does Not Apply (N = 180): 41%

ASSAULT: THREATS AT WORK

16. Have you ever been approached in a threatening manner by a parent while at work?

Yes (N = 240): 55%
No (N = 168): 39%
Does Not Apply (N = 27): 6%

17. Have you ever been approached in a threatening manner by a colleague while at work?

Yes (N = 111): 26%

No (N = 315): 72%

Does Not Apply (N = 9): 2%

18. Have you ever been approached in a threatening manner by an administrator while at work?

Yes (N = 120): 27%

No (N = 312): 72%

Does Not Apply (N = 3): 1%

19. Have you ever been approached in a threatening manner by one or more students while at work?

Yes (N = 279): 64%

No (N = 150): 35%

Does Not Apply (N = 6): 1%

ASSAULT: ONLINE THREATS AND BULLYING

20. In your opinion, have you ever been assaulted online because of your actions in education?

Yes (N = 99): 23%

No (N = 304): 74%

Does Not Apply (N = 12): 3%

21. Have you ever been the subject of social media bullying by a colleague?

Yes (N = 36): 8%

No (N = 396): 91%

Does Not Apply (N = 3): 1%

22. Have you ever been the subject of social media bullying by an administrator?

Yes (N = 12): 3%

No (N = 417): 96%

Does Not Apply (N = 6): 1%

23. Have you ever been the subject of social media bullying by a parent?

Yes (N = 87): 20%

No (N = 345): 79%

Does Not Apply (N = 3): 1%

24. Have you ever been the object of social media bullying by one or more students?

Yes (N = 51): 12%

No: (N = 375): 86%

Does Not Apply: (N = 9): 2%

ASSAULT: VERBAL

25. Have you ever been verbally assaulted because of your gender?
    Yes (N = 90): 21%
    No (N = 336): 77%
    Does Not Apply (N = 9): 2%
26. Have you ever been verbally assaulted by one or more students?
    Yes (N = 279): 64%
    No (N = 150): 35%
    Does Not Apply (N = 6): 1%
27. Have you ever been verbally assaulted by one or more administrators?
    Yes (N = 129): 29%
    No (N = 303): 70%
    Does Not Apply (N = 3): 1%
28. If you have been verbally assaulted by a colleague while at work, please specify from the list below.
    Yes (by fellow educator) (N = 87): 20%
    Yes (by administrator) (N = 87): 20%
    Yes (by both fellow teacher and administrator) (N = 15): 3%
    Yes (by counselor) (N = 0): 0%
    Yes (by coach) (N = 3): 1%
    Yes (by educational specialist) (N = 6): 1%
    Does Not Apply (N = 237): 55%
    Other (please specify) (N = 0): 0%
29. Have you ever been verbally assaulted by a parent during or after work in education?
    Yes, during work (N = 186): 43%
    Yes, after work (N = 21): 5%
    Yes, during work and after work (N = 63): 14%
    No (N = 156): 36%
    Does Not Apply (N = 9): 2%
30. If you are also a coach where you work, have you ever been assaulted verbally by a parent?
    Yes (N = 39): 9%
    No (N = 120): 28%
    Does Not Apply (N = 276): 63%

ASSAULT: PHYSICAL

31. Have you been purposefully spit at or on by one or more students?
    Yes (N = 105): 24%
    No (N = 288): 66%

One or more events were deemed accidents/incidents (N = 12): 3%
Does Not Apply (N = 30): 7%

32. Have you been purposefully kicked by one or more students?
    Yes (N = 147): 34%
    No (N = 267): 61%
    One or more events were deemed accidents/incidents (N = 6): 1%
    Does Not Apply (N = 15): 4%

33. Have you ever had objects thrown at you by one or more students?
    Yes (N = 201): 46%
    No (N = 219): 50%
    One or more events were deemed accidents/incidents (N = 9): 2%
    Does Not Apply (N = 6): 2%

34. Have you ever been physically assaulted by one or more students?
    Yes (N = 180): 41%
    No (N = 231): 53%
    One or more events were deemed accidents/incidents (N = 15): 4%
    Does Not Apply (N = 9): 2%

35. Have you ever been physically assaulted by a colleague while at work?
    Yes (by fellow teacher) (N = 10): 2%
    Yes (by fellow college or university educator) (N = 3): 1%
    Yes (by administrator) (N = 3): 1%
    Yes (by both fellow teacher and administrator) (N = 0): 0%
    Yes (by counselor) (N = 0): 0%
    Yes (by coach) (N = 0): 0%
    Yes (by educational specialist) (N = 0): 0%
    No (N = 417): 96%
    Other (please specify) (N = 0): 0%

36. If you are also a coach at the school where you are employed, have you ever been assaulted physically by a parent?
    Yes (N = 9): 2%
    No (N = 171): 39%
    Does Not Apply (N = 255): 59%

ASSAULT: SEXUAL

37. Have you ever experienced sexual advances or sexual pressure from one or more students?
    Yes, by face-to-face contact while at work (N = 36): 8%
    Yes, by face-to-face contact while away from work (N = 0): 0%
    Yes, by technology contact while at work (N = 0): 0%
    Yes, by technology contact while away from work (N = 3): 1%

Yes, by both face-to-face contact and technology contact while at work (N = 9): 2%

Yes, by both face-to-face contact and technology contact while away from work (N = 6): 1%

No (N = 372): 86%

Does Not Apply (N = 9): 2%

38. Have you ever experienced sexual advances or sexual pressure from a colleague?

Yes, by face-to-face contact while at work (N = 39): 9%

Yes, by face-to-face contact while away from work (N = 3): 1%

Yes, by technology contact while at work (N = 0): 0%

Yes, by technology contact while away from work (N = 3): 1%

Yes, by both face-to-face contact and technology contact while at work (N = 6): 1%

Yes, by both face-to-face contact and technology contact while away from work (N = 9): 2%

No (N = 366): 84%

Does Not Apply (N = 9): 2%

39. Have you ever experienced sexual advances or sexual pressure from an administrator?

Yes, by face-to-face contact while at work (N = 6): 1%

Yes, by face-to-face contact while away from work (N = 0): 0%

Yes, by technology contact while at work (N = 0): 0%

Yes, by technology contact while away from work (N = 6): 1%

Yes, by both face-to-face contact and technology contact while at work (N = 3): 1%

Yes, by both face-to-face contact and technology contact while away from work (N = 0): 0%

No (N = 408): 94%

Does Not Apply (N = 12): 3%

40. Have you ever experienced sexual advances or sexual pressure from a parent?

Yes, by face-to-face contact while at work (N = 24): 6%

Yes, by face-to-face contact while away from work (N = 6): 1%

Yes, by technology contact while at work (N = 0): 0%

Yes, by technology contact while away from work (N = 3): 1%

Yes, by both face-to-face contact and technology contact while at work (N = 3): 1%

Yes, by both face-to-face contact and technology contact while away from work (N = 6): 1%

No (N = 384): 88%

Does Not Apply (N = 9): 2%

ASSAULT: PERSONAL PROPERTY DAMAGE

41. Have you ever had any of your personal property damaged by students while at work?

Yes (N = 217): 61%

No (N = 141): 33%

Something was damaged but uncertain how damage occurred (N = 21): 5%

Does Not Apply (N = 6): 1%

42. Have you ever had any of your personal property damaged by parents while at work?

Yes (N = 9): 2%

No (N = 399): 92%

Something was damaged but uncertain how damage occurred (N = 12): 3%

Does Not Apply (N = 15): 3%

43. Have you ever had any of your personal property damaged by students while at home?

Yes (N = 27): 6%

No (N = 381): 88%

Something was damaged but uncertain how damage occurred (N = 15): 3%

Does Not Apply (N = 12): 3%

44. Have you ever had any of your personal property damaged by parents while at home?

Yes (N = 0): 0%

No (N = 405): 93%

Something was damaged but uncertain how damage occurred (N = 15): 4%

Does Not Apply (N = 15): 3%

45. Please feel free to share any additional anecdotal information* about your experiences or your colleagues' experiences as victims of assault. You may post these experiences here, or you may do so directly to erniezarraphd@aol.com.

*The following section includes a brief summarization of several of the anecdotes shared as write-in responses to this survey question.

- Student offered sexual favors for a better grade.
- As a male teacher, I have not experienced nearly as much of what you include in this survey compared to what my female colleagues have experienced. This is probably because I am a male, 250 pounds, and a former professional hockey player.
- Educators' rights exist but are not enforced.

- Educators have no rights and are subjected to so very much.
- My iPhone was stolen at work. I know who took it, and he knows I know. But nothing was done.
- I know several teachers who have been verbally attacked or physically attacked by students.
- I started teaching at age forty-two and was surprised at the sexual advances by students toward me. I am now fifty-seven, and the advances have slowed, but still they persist.
- When I was a student in high school, in the 1970s, one of my high school male teachers was a sexual predator and made sexual advances toward me frequently. It sickens me that he worked in education for some forty years and retired "well-respected."
- I am in the middle of a lawsuit from a high-profile national case. I was one of the teachers who was knocked unconscious while trying to break up a fight at my school.
- The students who were assaulting me were assaulting others, including students. I was bothered that I could not provide a safe environment for my students.
- I have had colleagues cyberbullied online by students through social media and by tagging at our school.
- It is the educators who want to be "friends" with students and today's parents who cause much of the trouble these days.
- My district has a restraining order against a parent due to verbal abuse and threatened physical assault. I was physically assaulted by another teacher. Despite three witnesses and several other complaints against the teacher, our administration called it a "personality conflict." The same teacher in question was eventually fired, and I was moved to another school.
- I am a Christian school administrator, and I am less likely to encounter these problems. I taught and coached in the public schools without overt problems. I'm six-foot-five, 270 pounds, and athletic.
- I know of administrators cursing up storms and yelling at teachers at the tops of their voices while their office doors are closed. The front office was walking on eggshells.
- Once, a student threatened to smoke me. He was removed from the classroom but continued to harass me. I filed an official report, but the student was not removed from the school. Later that same year, the student assaulted and seriously injured another teacher.

Index

About the Author

Ernest J. Zarra III, teaches college preparatory U.S. government and politics and economics classes to seniors at the state-decorated and top-ranked Centennial High School in Bakersfield, California. Zarra has earned five degrees and holds a PhD in teaching and learning theory from the University of Southern California, with cognates in psychology and technology. He is a former Christian College First-Team All-American soccer player and former teacher of the year for the prestigious Fruitvale School District and was awarded Top Graduate Student in Education from California State University at Bakersfield.

Dr. Zarra has written eight books, including the following Rowman & Littlefield publications: (1) *The Teacher Exodus: Reversing the Trend and Keeping Teachers in the Classroom*, (2) *The Entitled Generation: Helping Teachers Teach and Reach the Minds and Hearts of Generation Z* (2017), (3) *Helping Parents Understand the Minds and Hearts of Generation Z* (2017), (4) *Common Sense Education: From Common Core to ESSA and Beyond* (2016), (5) *The Wrong Direction for Today's Schools: The Impact of Common Core on American Education* (2015), and (6) *Teacher-Student Relationships: Crossing into the Emotional, Physical, and Sexual Realms* (2013). His book *The Wrong Direction for Today's Schools* was the award-winning 2016 Choice Outstanding Academic Title.

Zarra has written more than a dozen professional journal articles, developed curriculum, and served as a professional development leader and facilitator for the largest high school district in California, the Kern High School District. He also assists school districts as an educational consultant, leads seminars on classroom management and instructional methods, and presents at professional education conferences. He is a member in good standing of the National Education Association, California Teachers Association, the

Association for Supervision and Curriculum Development, American Educational Research Association, and several national honor societies, including Kappa Delta Pi.

Ernie is originally from Bloomfield, New Jersey, and is married to Suzi, also an educator. They have two adult children and have resided in California most of their adult lives.